TANKMASTER

An essential guide to keeping
GOLDFISH

BERNICE BREWSTER

INTERPET PUBLISHING

Author

Bernice Brewster first became interested in fish as a child, accompanying her grandfather on fishing trips. After graduating from London University, she worked for the Fish Section of the Natural History Museum before moving to a company dealing in Japanese Koi. She now runs an aquatic consultancy. In addition to writing articles for fishkeeping magazines, she has also contributed papers to scientific and veterinary journals on aspects of fish husbandry and management.

Consultant: Dennis Roberts, Nationwide and G.S.G.B. judge.

© 2003 Interpet Publishing,
Vincent Lane, Dorking, Surrey, RH4 3YX, England.
All rights reserved.
ISBN: 1-903098-34-3

Credits
Created and designed: Ideas into Print,
Box Cottage, Claydon, Suffolk IP6 0AB, England.
Production management: Consortium, Poslingford,
Suffolk CO10 8RA, England.
Print production: Sino Publishing House Ltd., Hong Kong.
Printed and bound in China.

Below: The flash of bright colour as pond goldfish come to the surface to feed is one of the many pleasures of keeping these elegant fish.

Contents

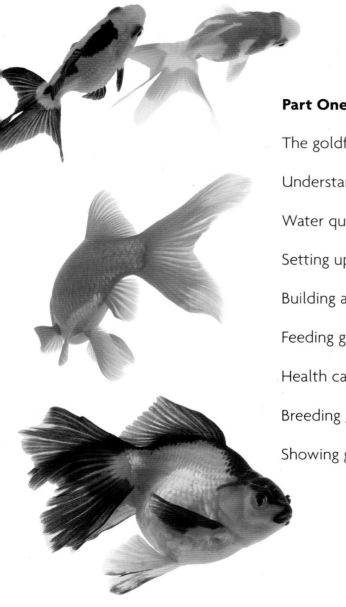

Young multicoloured orandas add variety and movement to a planted aquarium.

Part One

A pet with pedigree

For many hobbyists, the first introduction to keeping fish as pets is through owning goldfish. They are sometimes regarded as rather humble compared with colourful tropical freshwater and marine fish species, and often people will admit to keeping 'only goldfish' as though they are not quite fashionable. However, the truth is that no other species of fish enjoys the remarkable ancestry and popularity of the goldfish.

Despite the range of shapes and colours, all goldfish belong to a single species, *Carassius auratus*. The natural, or wild, type is actually bronze on top and, when young, yellow underneath. As adults they turn a deep orange-red colour, which may give a clue to the origins of the domesticated varieties. Goldfish originated in the Far East;

the fish commonly found wild in ponds and streams throughout Europe are the offspring of escaped or liberated ornamental varieties. The fact that these introduced fish have reverted to their wild colour is testament to the selective breeding programmes required to produce the sparkling orange-gold body colour, characteristic of the common goldfish.

It seems that the first goldfish to arrive in Europe came from China into England at about the end of the seventeenth century. Drawings of the two 'natural curiosities' appear in a catalogue dated 1705. The fact that these goldfish were still alive on arrival in England is evidence of their hardiness, as the journey would have taken several months under very stressful conditions for

the fish. However, it was another 150 years or so before goldfish became popular as pet fish. During the 1850s, Victorians kept goldfish in glass bowls in the parlour, but still regarded them as an exotic species.

A number of fancy varieties of goldfish, such as veiltails, fantails and even egg fish were imported into Europe from about 1860, but it was only after the Second World War that the more delicate fancy varieties became readily available through the availability of insulated boxes and more efficient air transportation. It is really no wonder that the goldfish has earned a special place in fishkeeping and while this book will examine the popular varieties and how to keep and enjoy them, it is really a celebration of a very special fish!

THE GOLDFISH HOBBY

The goldfish is probably the most popular pet fish in the world; there can be very few countries where it has not been introduced. Although we know that the goldfish species *(Carassius auratus)* is native to China, there are very few clues to tell us when it was first domesticated. One thing is certain: while the history of goldfish development may appear quite disjointed and uncertain, no other fish has a pedigree dating back for over 1,000 years.

There are some delightful stories concerning the origins of the goldfish, not least in the book Shu I Chi, the Record of Stories and Marvels. According to this tale, in the reign of the Emperor P'ing in 769 B.C. there was a drought for 100 days. When sacrifices were made to appease the gods, a well appeared, a goldfish jumped out and the rains fell.

The common, or ancestral, goldfish

Chinese books contain an assortment of references to red or golden fish from the beginning of time, but true authentication of the existence of the goldfish appears during the Sung Dynasty (960-1279 A.D.). After this period, there are increasing references to the goldfish in Chinese literature, the origins of its popularity as a pet. During the eleventh century, goldfish breeders were improving their stock and

able to produce the gold colour with which we are familiar. At this time, keeping chi, the Chinese name for goldfish, was preferable to keeping li, or carp. Whether this was the common carp *(Cyprinus carpio)* seems to be debatable. By the end of the thirteenth century, goldfish of many types were sold in profitable numbers as domestic pets at Chinese markets. Chi were kept in shallow bowls that were highly decorated on the outside, but left plain white on the inside. Each bowl housed just two fish, or even one individual, and the fish were viewed from above. This supposedly led to the

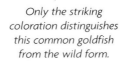

Only the striking coloration distinguishes this common goldfish from the wild form.

Right: Exhibiting goldfish in competitive shows is an integral part of the hobby. For some, it is a consuming passion, with a great deal of time and effort spent on breeding the best specimens of particular varieties.

development of a variety of goldfish with the characteristic of the eyes looking upward towards the observer – often the opulent and most vain aristocracy. It is documented that these goldfish with upward-looking eyes were the ancestral forms of the celestial and bubble-eye variations, and the origin of the fancy varieties. However, there is no documented evidence to suggest when the first varieties of fancy goldfish were developed from the common goldfish, more correctly known as the 'ancestral goldfish'.

Fancy goldfish

In 1200, we find the first reference to fancy goldfish – fish with snow-white, lustrous bodies and black spots called 'tortoiseshell fish'. After this, there is no further reference to fancy goldfish until the latter

part of the Ming Dynasty (1368-1644), when a large number of multicoloured varieties are mentioned, with exotic names such as 'Golden Helmets', 'Piled-up Gold', 'Inlaid Jade', 'Flowing Water', 'Lotus Terrace' and 'Eight Melon Seeds'.

The development of fancy varieties of goldfish continued with the egg fish, fantails and ryukin (the latter gave rise to the veiltail) that appeared in the sixteenth century. By the seventeenth century, a whole range of goldfish of different colours was being bred in quantity. The celestial and bubble-eye did not appear until the eighteenth century. The origins of the celestial are shrouded in mystery, with some suggestion that this variety was obtained by the Chinese from Korea.

Everyone is attracted to the fancy varieties of goldfish, such as this young metallic fantail.

Selective breeding

Breeding fancy goldfish became a major industry throughout China and Japan, where whole villages would be dedicated to the production and refinement of a single variety. The techniques of successful breeding and rearing were handed down from grandfather to father to son and thus each goldfish strain would become highly refined. Much of this knowledge is retained within the generations of these specialist breeders and will remain forever part of the 'mystery' that is the goldfish.

Many commercial and hobbyist breeders have dedicated their lives to developing hardy strains of fancy goldfish by attempting to emulate the genetic refinement resulting from highly selective breeding, but there is no doubt that the hard work of the early Chinese goldfish farmers created the foundations on which the hobby rests.

Modern fancy goldfish

A multitude of fancy varieties has been developed from the humble beginnings of the ancestral goldfish; indeed, it is thought that over 120 varieties of fancy goldfish have been developed and each season brings with it new and sometimes (though not always) highly attractive varieties. Firstly, the tail fin became paired, and in some cases, the lack of a dorsal fin, skyward-looking eyes, or both, were developed as a characteristic. Additional characteristics, such as the fluffy 'hood' prized by enthusiasts of the oranda, lionhead and ranchu, also became popular.

At the same time, variations in colouring have been developed, with the result that goldfish varieties now range from matt black through blue, chocolate brown and orange-speckled to silver with a scarlet 'cap'. It is not unusual to see goldfish with an attractive red-and-silver, or sarasa, colouring. This has traditionally been the popular colouring of the comet (a variety of goldfish with a single tail that is ideally three-quarters the length of the body).

In addition to colour, fish with different scale types have been developed. One of the most notable is the pearlscale, which has convex or domed scales. These, combined with a virtually spherical body shape, give the fish the appearance of an oversized golf ball.

Recent introductions include the panda butterfly, a black-and-silver fancy goldfish with globe-shaped eyes and a tail resembling a butterfly.

A panda butterfly, aptly named for its black-and-silver colour pattern and butterfly tail.

The divided tail fin has forked lobes that take on the shape of a butterfly.

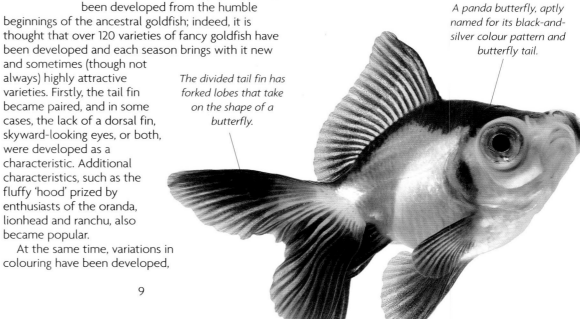

The Japanese have successfully developed the jikin (pronounced jee-kin). This all-silver, metallic-scaled variety has the body shape of the ancestral goldfish and a most attractive red colouring, ideally restricted to the fins and lips. In the best examples, the tail fins are butterfly shaped and perpendicular to the body when viewed from above.

Traditionally, the most popular fancy goldfish varieties in the West have been the veiltail, oranda, fantail and moor and their derivatives.

Below: This view of a jikin highlights the main ornamental feature of the variety – the tail. The upper and lower lobes are flattened and resemble a butterfly or a peacock with its wings outstretched.

Cultural icons

In China, goldfish were so highly revered in the past that they still retain a special place in the hearts of the people today. To the Chinese, goldfish represent wealth and prosperity, and any business owner who wants to ensure success in their own enterprise will keep a collection of fancy goldfish on the premises. Individuals keep goldfish in jars as a good luck charm, and even today, fancy goldfish are sold in their hundreds from round barrels in market places throughout China.

Given such a passion for goldfish, it is only natural that icons are available in many forms, from porcelain jars and urns (some of which resemble those early goldfish bowls) to artworks, embroidery and weavings. Reproductions of goldfish art are relatively inexpensive, while collectors will pay dearly for genuine antiques depicting fancy goldfish.

The ryukin is a Japanese fancy goldfish with a characteristic hump behind the head.

The goldfish hobby today

The popularity of the goldfish should not be underestimated, whether they are kept in the garden pond or in the aquarium. Although a goldfish pond is probably part of the garden design, it is normal for the fish to be individually recognised and identified by name. Owners take great delight in tapping the side of the pond, which is the signal for feeding, and the surface of the water literally boils with hungry goldfish, shubunkins and comets. Goldfish in the aquarium are also treasured pets for both children and adults, but these are more likely to be the fancy varieties. The favourite fancy varieties include the veiltail, oranda, moor, fantail, pearlscale and lionhead. For dedicated hobbyists, the list of varieties is much greater, although many will restrict their interest to just one or two. Nevertheless, many goldfish hobbyists are probably just as interested in good-quality common goldfish, shubunkins and comets as they are in the more 'specialist' varieties.

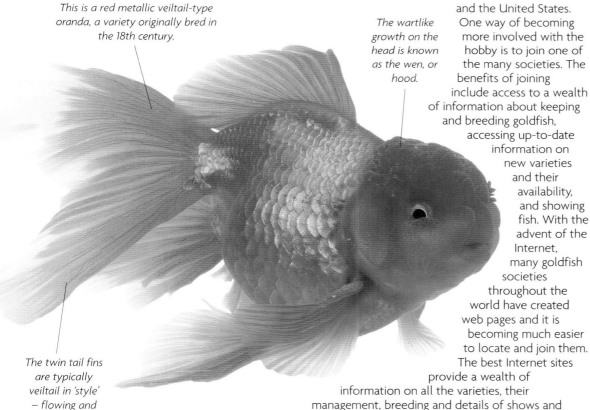

This is a red metallic veiltail-type oranda, a variety originally bred in the 18th century.

The wartlike growth on the head is known as the wen, or hood.

The twin tail fins are typically veiltail in 'style' – flowing and graceful.

Traditionally, China and Japan have been the source of common and fancy varieties of goldfish, although Italy, America and Israel produce large numbers of common goldfish using intensive aquaculture techniques. The export market for all these countries remains strong because interest in goldfish keeping is a worldwide hobby, with a great following in Europe and the United States. One way of becoming more involved with the hobby is to join one of the many societies. The benefits of joining include access to a wealth of information about keeping and breeding goldfish, accessing up-to-date information on new varieties and their availability, and showing fish. With the advent of the Internet, many goldfish societies throughout the world have created web pages and it is becoming much easier to locate and join them. The best Internet sites provide a wealth of information on all the varieties, their management, breeding and details of shows and other activities. Hobbyists commonly join and communicate with other clubs throughout the world via the Internet and by email.

The goldfish also plays a huge role in the commercial side of the hobby, generating massive sales annually, in addition to the associated 'dry' goods such as liners, glassfibre and plastic ponds, aquariums, pumps, filters, health remedies and food.

The popularity of the goldfish and all the fancy varieties has increased over the years and no doubt will continue to do so, as they hold such a special place in the history of fishkeeping.

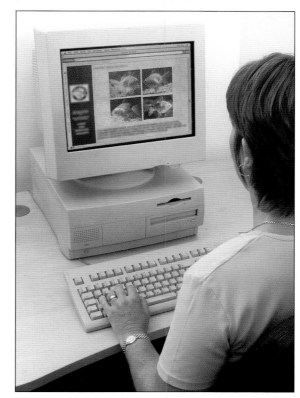

Above: *Using email and accessing the Internet are excellent ways of keeping in touch with hobbyists around the world and for gathering information from websites set up by clubs and societies.*

UNDERSTANDING GOLDFISH

Most of us could describe what a goldfish looks like, but many questions remain: what do the fins do, why does it have scales, can it hear? In other words, how does a goldfish work? The photograph and notes shown opposite cover the basic anatomy of goldfishes and provide an insight into the main body systems they share with most fish. From the hobbyist's point of view, the important aspects centre around how the fish looks, which is not only a question of its body shape and fins, but also its scale arrangement and colour. At this point, we need to look more closely at the skin and scales.

The structure of the skin

The outermost layer of the skin is called the epidermis and is a living tissue that forms a very fine coating over the outside of the scales. If you have ever touched a goldfish, you will know that you can feel the scales and sense the delicate nature of this outer layer. This is why you should always handle goldfish with wet hands because our dry skin sticks to the epidermis and literally tears it. The epidermis is responsible for producing a layer of mucus, which has two functions: firstly, it acts as a lubricant to help the goldfish swim through the water and secondly, it provides a protective barrier against parasites, bacteria and viruses.

Immediately beneath the epidermis is a layer of skin called the dermis, which is where the cells responsible for producing colours are formed. These are either chromatophores or iridocytes. The chromatophores produce 'true' colour patterns and are named according to the colour they create –

The basic design

Goldfish have a good sense of hearing. The internal ears are located at the back of the head, close to the base of the skull. A series of modified vertebrae connect them to the gas-filled swimbladder – a buoyancy organ – which amplifies the perceived sound.

Along the middle of the body a line of perforated scales marks the position of a sensory system called the lateral line. This can detect small changes in water pressure, giving goldfish awareness of other fish and the sudden movement of a predator.

Powerful muscles down either side of the body pull the tail, or caudal fin, from side to side to provide forward propulsion.

Ears at base of skull

Lateral line

Dorsal fin

Caudal peduncle

Tail, or caudal fin

Gills beneath this cover

Pectoral fin

Pelvic fin

Anal fin

Goldfish extract oxygen from the water through the gills. The gill filaments contain tiny capillaries in close contact with the water, allowing the blood to collect oxygen and release carbon dioxide. Goldfish excrete most of their nitrogenous waste as ammonia from the gills. Only a small amount of nitrogenous waste is shed as very dilute urine.

Two sets of paired fins, the pectoral and pelvic fins, also keep goldfish stable as they move through the water. They prevent rolling but also stop the head from pitching up and down.

As goldfish swim, the dorsal and anal fins are used to prevent the body from rolling sideways. Alert goldfish, such as when they are being fed, hold the dorsal and anal fins stiffly upright, ready to swim away quickly.

erythrophores (orange and red), xanthophores (yellow), melanophores (black) and leucophores (white). There are pigment granules in the cells that can spread out or contract, altering the strength of colour in the skin. (Sick fish become paler because the pigments shrink within the chromatophores.) The colour patterns found in goldfish varieties are produced by the number, arrangement and colour of the chromatophores in the skin, and the intensity is a result of the extension or contraction of the pigment granules within them. Colour is affected by environmental conditions (including temperature) and by the age of the fish, so it is common for the colours to change, which in turn may affect the quality of any show goldfish.

The reflective, metallic 'finish' of the skin is created by iridocytes, which contain crystals like tiny mirrors. These contain silvery guanine and cannot shrink or expand, like other pigment cells.

Colours and scale patterns

There are two groups of colour in goldfish: metallic and calico. Metallic refers to the structure of the dermis, where there is a layer of iridocytes that contain guanine. Metallic fish include single-coloured goldfish and those with combinations of two or more colours, which should be strong and bright.

Calico fish have three scale patterns: reflective, where there is guanine present; nacreous, where the guanine layer is only partially present; and matt, where the guanine is absent. In the calico varieties of goldfish, the depth of the pigment cells in the dermis give rise to the coloration, but blue, white (silver), red and black – and sometimes other colours, such as violet or brown – are also present. In calico fish it is important that the reds are really bright and the black is a sooty colour.

The structure of scales

The scales are formed in the dermis and are bony plates that overlap like tiles on a roof. Under the microscope, the scales can be seen to have a series of rings, rather like those found inside the trunk of a tree, and similarly, the rings can be used to age the fish. During the warmer months of the year, when food is readily available and temperatures are high, goldfish grow rapidly and the rings are quite spaced out. In the winter, the fish feeds less and the water temperature is low, so there is little growth and the rings become tightly packed. By counting the tightly packed zones, we can estimate the age of the goldfish, a process known as 'reading scales'. This is easier in pond goldfish, which are subject to seasonal temperature fluctuations; in the aquarium, the constant conditions make the structure of the rings much more even and difficult to read.

Sometimes during handling or spawning, scales may be knocked off, but the cells in the dermis very quickly replace the missing ones. These replacement scales do not have any growth rings, which only start to appear once the scales have rapidly grown to the same size as the others and growth slows down again to create the zones of tightly packed rings.

Right: *The scales overlap each other, forming a protective layer over the body of the fish. The pitted scales of the lateral line system are also clearly shown here.*

Scale types in goldfish

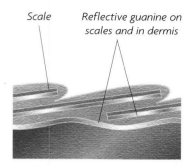

Scale / Reflective guanine on scales and in dermis

Metallic scales

Layers of iridocytes (guanine crystals) beneath each scale and in the dermis itself give the goldfish its characteristic metallic sheen.

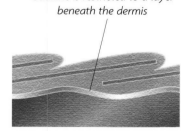

Guanine is restricted to a layer beneath the dermis

Nacreous scales

Here, iridocytes are just present in the dermis and can only shine through a limited amount, giving a 'mother of pearl' appearance.

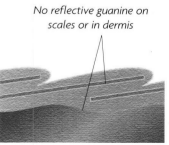

No reflective guanine on scales or in dermis

Matt scales

With no iridocytes beneath the scales or in the dermis, scales appear to be transparent and the coloration is provided by pigment cells alone.

It is very common for hobbyists to test the water in an aquarium or pond before stocking it with any goldfish. In most instances, the water quality is good and the fishkeeper adds the goldfish, but this is exactly when the water conditions begin to deteriorate, as it is the fish themselves that pollute the water. Goldfish produce nitrogenous waste, largely in the form of ammonia, which is excreted through the gills. Only a small amount of urea is shed in the form of very dilute urine. The ammonia is poisonous to the goldfish and the function of

How nitrogen is cycled in nature

Fish consume plants and other nitrogen-containing foods and excrete nitrogenous waste.

Ammonia (NH_3) is the main waste product and is excreted from the gills and in lower concentrations in urine.

Bacteria living in the substrate convert toxic ammonia to nitrite (NO_2), still poisonous to fish.

Plants use nitrates as a food source and incorporate the nitrogen into proteins that in turn are eaten by fish and other creatures.

Different bacteria 'feed' on nitrite and produce nitrate (NO_3) – a much less harmful substance.

the biological filter is to break down the waste, firstly into nitrite and then into nitrate through the action of bacteria and other micro-organisms associated with the nitrogen cycle. Nitrite is also poisonous to goldfish, but the final breakdown product – nitrate – is less harmful and a useful fertiliser for aquatic plants. To keep the water free of ammonia and nitrite, the filtration system should run continuously throughout the year, although obviously it needs to be turned off for brief periods to allow any maintenance to take place. However, if carried out correctly this will not have any detrimental effect on the beneficial bacteria.

Above: *To test water for nitrite level, add the required number of reagent drops to a measured sample and shake gently.*

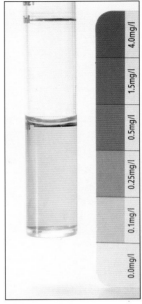

Right: *Compare the colour change in the sample to a printed chart to read off the nitrite concentration.*

Testing the water

In a new pond or aquarium, there are insufficient bacteria in the filtration system to fulfil the important role of breaking down the nitrogenous waste produced by the goldfish. In the first few weeks of establishing the aquarium or pond, first ammonia and then nitrite can pollute the water, causing the goldfish to become sick, or even die. It is important to monitor the water for the presence of ammonia or nitrite using test kits, which are easy to use and available from aquatic retailers. If either ammonia or nitrite are polluting the water in the aquarium or pond, carry out regular partial water changes, using treated tapwater.

Tapwater or rainwater?

People often believe that it is better to collect rainwater for topping up the pond. However, the problem with rainwater is that the atmosphere is laden with the greenhouse gas carbon dioxide, which readily dissolves into it as the rain falls through the air. The dissolved carbon dioxide in the rainwater makes the water mildly acidic and it becomes increasingly so as it comes into contact with other airborne pollutants, such as nitrogen oxide emissions

Below: Rainwater is naturally mildly acidic and as it runs over the roof and through the guttering, it can become contaminated with various substances harmful to fish.

from cars. The acidified rainwater then comes into contact with nails, screws and other metalwork associated with roofs and sheds, and a small amount of these metals are dissolved into the water, which then finds its way into the water butt at the end of the pipe. The final result is water that is mildly acidic and potentially contains toxic metals in solution, which is not good for goldfish.

On the other hand, tapwater contains a variety of minerals that are actually used by goldfish but missing from rainwater. So even though it is necessary to treat tapwater with a water conditioner to remove harmful chlorine disinfectants, it is still a safer option than rainwater in an aquarium or pond.

Oxygen levels in the pond

In the garden pond during the summer, oxygen gas is largely insoluble in the warm water, but this is just the time of year when the goldfish are most active and their consumption of this vital gas is greatest. In planted ponds, large numbers of submerged aquatic plants will compete overnight with the goldfish for oxygen, leading to overnight depletion. In extreme cases, the largest or most active fish in the pond are found dead first thing in the morning. It is important to ensure that the pond is adequately aerated; the continuous operation of the filtration system will help, but it may be necessary to keep water features such as waterfalls or fountains running overnight during periods of very hot or sultry weather.

Diffusers, commonly known as airstones, attached to airlines.

Left: An airpump in use. The diffusers force the air into small bubbles that readily deliver oxygen to the water in the pond. Keep this simple kit handy for emergencies.

Above: Fountains disturb the water surface by splashing and creating a rippling effect that helps to aerate the water. Fish may cluster beneath them on hot summer days.

Most people probably associate goldfish with round bowls, a little gravel, a castle or some other ornament and, occasionally, a scrap of aquatic plant, such as Canadian pondweed (Elodea canadensis). Often, there is no aeration or filtration, and every couple of weeks, the unfortunate goldfish is extracted from the bowl and placed in a bucket or jug, while the water in the bowl is discarded and replaced with unconditioned tapwater. Between these water changes, the goldfish is often seen at the surface, gasping for air, especially if its bowl has been placed close to a radiator or window and the warmth prevents vital oxygen from dissolving into the water. This poor goldfish, living in its unfiltered and poorly aerated bowl, is in a permanent state of stress and, not very surprisingly, probably only survives for a few years, whereas the lifespan of the common variety is easily 20-25 years.

Sizes and capacities of standard tanks

Tank	Volume	Weight of water
60x30x30cm (24x12x12in)	55 litres (12 gallons)	55kg (120lbs)
60x30x38cm (24x12x15in)	68 litres (15 gallons)	68kg (150lbs)
90x30x30cm (36x12x12in)	82 litres (18 gallons)	82kg (180lbs)
90x30x38cm (36x12x15in)	104 litres (23 gallons)	104kg (230lbs)
120x30x30cm (48x12x12in)	109 litres (24 gallons)	109kg (240lbs)
120x30x38cm (48x12x15in)	136 litres (30 gallons)	136kg (300lbs)

Choosing a tank

The best way to keep many of the fancy varieties of goldfish is in an aquarium, and you can choose from a range of different sizes. Aim for a minimum tank size of 60x30x30cm (24x12x12in), although it is better to select the largest aquarium you can afford and accommodate; goldfish thrive where they have plenty of space.

Local newspapers can be a good source of inexpensive aquariums, but be aware that secondhand tanks could be faulty. Even though they may be equipped with pumps or filtration systems, the fittings could be old, worn or even leaking. New tanks are usually covered by a guarantee period, should anything go wrong, so this is probably the safest way to buy a first aquarium. It is also best to invest in a purpose-built stand or cabinet on which to place the aquarium. Once filled with water, it will be very heavy and most pieces of household furniture are not designed to carry such a load. Stands or cabinets are also helpful in raising the aquarium to a height at which children can view the fish but are prevented from damaging the tank glass.

Siting the aquarium

Siting the aquarium in the correct place is very important, and a firm foundation is essential to support its weight. If the flooring is constructed of concrete, there is little problem with regard to the weight, but if it is covered with tiles or carpet, it is a good idea to use a flat piece of metal or other suitable material under each leg of the stand to spread the load and prevent the floor covering from being flattened. Where the aquarium is sited on a wooden floor, spread the load over the floor joists. Always avoid the centre of the room, where the load-bearing capacity of the floor is at its weakest.

Apart from the weight of the filled aquarium, there are other important factors to consider when choosing the ideal spot for your aquarium. Avoid placing it close to windows, or even in the conservatory, where the sun will cause the water temperature to rise significantly during the day and drop rapidly at night. In the winter months, despite advances in the effectiveness of double-glazing, low outside temperatures may still cool the water in the aquarium. The natural light from the windows can also be intense and may even promote the growth of nuisance algae.

Hallways and sites adjacent to doors are also poor locations for the aquarium, as they tend to be draughty, and the frequent passage of people will disturb the goldfish. In many instances, the corners of a room are an ideal location and often this is where the power supply can be found. Try to avoid trailing cables around the room; it is both unsightly and a hazard.

Purpose-built aquarium cabinets have the space so that the electrical connections to filters and other equipment can be installed inside them. This is both tidy and safe, since it reduces the likelihood of electrical wiring coming into contact with water. Electricity and water make a dangerous combination. In any case, it is a good idea to fit a Residual Current Device (RCD) onto the plugs supplying the aquarium. This will cut electricity to the system if there is a short circuit.

Avoid siting an aquarium in a bedroom, as the noise of the pumps and bubbling water is quite disturbing, although no doubt in the end you can become accustomed to these sounds. It is quite common for young children to want to keep goldfish in their room and no doubt it is tempting either not to fit the aquarium with the necessary airpump, airstones and filter or, alternatively, only to run them during the daytime. Both these options are unacceptable, as they will cause the water quality to deteriorate (see page 14).

Setting up the aquarium

Once you have chosen a site for the aquarium, assemble the stand or cabinet according to the manufacturer's directions. Place a plastic foam mat

Left: Remove any dust on the glass, otherwise it will leave a film on the water surface when the tank is filled. Clean the glass carefully inside and out, but avoid potentially harmful household chemicals.

or sheet of polystyrene, trimmed to the correct size, on the stand and set the aquarium on top of it. This cushioning prevents the tank from fracturing as a result of any tiny imperfection in the stand or support – even a small piece of grit can cause irreparable damage once the tank is full.

Use a spirit level to ensure that the aquarium is level. Many stands and cabinets have one or more adjustable legs, which can be used to compensate for any unevenness in the flooring. At this stage, it is a good idea to fill the tank with water, firstly to ensure that once filled it is still level, and secondly to check that it is watertight before setting it up with plants, ornaments and goldfish. Make any necessary adjustments to the levels after removing all or some of the water, otherwise the weight will make it difficult to alter the screw foot and could even damage the thread. If the tank is watertight, remove some of the water and clean the inside glass with a soft cloth. Do not use any household cleaners, as residues will be harmful to the goldfish. Discard the

Above: Use a spirit level from side to side and back to front to ensure that the stand is true. Test it again when the tank is in its final position. Mistakes are difficult to rectify later in the setting up process.

Left: Adjust the screw feet on each leg of the stand to ensure that everything is level. Ask a helper to hold the tank as you do this in case it is in danger of toppling over.

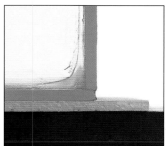

Right: As cushioning between the all-glass tank and its stand or cabinet, use a foam mat or a single sheet of polystyrene, cut slightly larger than the dimensions of the tank floor.

remaining water and clean the outside glass panels of the aquarium. You will be surprised by the amount of dust and the fingerprints on them; these are a complete distraction if not removed.

Adding the substrate

Gravel is usually chosen for the base of the aquarium, and there are many different types, from very brightly coloured ones through to jet black. The gravel should be inert, which means it should not react with the water in the aquarium. Always check that coloured gravels are suitable for use in aquariums; some types are designed purely for decoration and the dyes used are toxic to fish.

Substrates are available in various sizes. River sand is ideal for planting (best used as a layer with other substrates), but cannot be used with undergravel filters (see page 19). Fine gravel is also good for supporting plant growth and works well when mixed with larger grades. Medium-sized gravel is a good choice for most aquariums and can be used with undergravel filtration. The coarsest gravel, or pea shingle, is better for large aquarium systems and is often mixed with other gravels of different sizes to create a natural-looking substrate.

Never collect gravel from any natural sources, such as rivers or beaches, as there is always a risk of

River sand has rounded grains and is ideal for growing plants.

Coarse gravel is best for large tanks and can be mixed with medium gravel for a stream bed effect.

Coloured gravels are sold in single or mixed colours.

Fine gravel (also available in a lime-free form) looks good in smaller displays.

Medium gravel is suitable for most aquarium sizes and filter systems.

Black gravel shows up the fishes' colours and can also be mixed with paler substrates.

introducing pollutants. Even more importantly, disturbing the substrate in rivers could damage the breeding grounds or eggs of native fish species that spawn in clean gravel.

When you buy gravel, it is described as 'washed', but nonetheless, it is always very dusty and must be carefully cleaned before it is placed in the aquarium. Even rounded gravel can be quite rough on your skin, so take care when cleaning it. Use a wooden stick to agitate it to remove the dust, rather than your unprotected hands.

The depth of gravel in the aquarium rather depends on the type of filter system you install. For undergravel filters, the gravel bed should be about 6cm (2.4in) deep, otherwise a depth of 4-5 cm (1.6-2in) is ideal. If you are using an undergravel filter, fit the plastic base plates and uplift tubing before adding the gravel. When adding gravel to the aquarium do so a bit at a time, either in handfuls or using a plastic jug or container, pouring it close to the base. Avoid tipping the gravel from any height, as a sharp piece of stone could break the glass base of the aquarium.

Right: *Add the substrate carefully in handfuls or use a plastic measuring jug, taking care not to drop the gravel from a height.*

Installing the filters

A filter is an extremely important piece of equipment that will support beneficial bacteria and other micro-organisms that will break down the harmful wastes produced by goldfish (see page 14). There are three types of filter that can be used on the goldfish aquarium: undergravel, and external and internal power filters.

Undergravel Filters

Either internal or external power filters are really the best type of filtration to fit onto an aquarium these days, but the undergravel filter is possibly the best option for the bowl types of aquariums or small tanks. While not the perfect way of filtering a tank or bowl, it is better than no filtration at all. The base plate of the filter has slits and holes cut into the plastic and is raised above the floor of the aquarium, creating a small gap. This plate must be installed first, then the tube known as an uplift tube, and finally, the gravel can be spread on top. The undergravel filter works by drawing water through the holes in the plate and up the tube and spilling back into the aquarium at the top. The water is moved through the gravel, plate and uplift tube by means of either an airstone, connected by airline to an airpump, or by an electric water pump called a powerhead. If the airpump is lower than the water level in the

Left: The base plate and uplift tube of an undergravel filter. A powerhead draws water up the tube.

Right: The foam cartridge inside an internal power filter becomes colonised with beneficial bacteria. During maintenance, rinse it with tank water to remove the fine debris without affecting the bacteria.

aquarium, fit a one-way check valve into the airline to prevent water from siphoning into the airpump in the event of any loss of electrical power.

The problem with undergravel filters is that they are not particularly efficient and the organic waste is retained in the tank. Over a period of time, this clogs the filter system, resulting in deteriorating water quality and sick fish. Furthermore, most plants do not grow well where undergravel filtration is used, as they do not thrive in the constant flow of water around the roots.

External power filters

These are located outside the aquarium and work in the same way as internal power filters in that they pass the tank water through filter media and return it to the aquarium. A typical external power filter consists of a canister filled with filter media – usually arranged in layers or compartments that contain mechanical, biological and sometimes chemical media – with an electrically powered water pump at the top. Water drawn from the tank passes through the media canister and is returned, usually though a spraybar or other attachment to add air to the flow.

As with internal filters, it is important to keep any mechanical filter media clean to maintain the

Below: An external power filter contains a large volume of media to deal with the considerable waste generated by goldfish.

The intake pipe draws in water through a strainer.

This return pipe has a multi-directional flow.

Screw the taps onto the inlet and outlet ports of the motor housing. Make final adjustments with the filter in position.

efficient working of the filter. Always follow the manufacturer's directions carefully when installing any electrical equipment and if you are unsure, consult a qualified electrician.

Internal power filters

These operate inside the aquarium and are suitable for most tanks. Water is drawn through a filter medium – usually a foam cartridge – by means of a small electrical pump. The foam cartridge acts as a biological filtration system, providing a large surface area for beneficial bacteria and other micro-organisms to colonise and break down the waste produced by the goldfish. As the water is pumped back into the aquarium, it can be aerated by a pipe that draws in air from above the surface and mixes it with the returning water flow. Never run the pump

without water in the tank, as it will quickly burn out. Most manufacturers provide a guide to minimum water levels.

Bear in mind that if the foam cartridge becomes heavily soiled, the pump cannot draw enough water through the filter to keep it cool and, again, this will lead to pump failure. The best way to keep the foam cartridge clean is to rinse it gently in some of the aquarium water in a separate container. Avoid using tapwater, as it is treated with chlorine and chloramine, potent bactericides that can kill the bacteria in the biological filter, leading to water quality problems.

In addition to a foam cartridge, some internal filters also contain mechanical filter media, which strain out dirt particles. A compartment with a chemical medium, such as activated carbon,

removes toxins. Keep the mechanical filter media clean to ensure the free running of the pump and to allow the biological part of the filter to work efficiently.

Lighting the aquarium

Most aquariums these days are supplied with hoods and lighting already installed and it is simply a matter of plugging the system into the electrical supply.

Below: With the decor and plants (here, plastic) in place, install a hood. This prevents fish escaping and houses the lighting to illuminate the display. Fluorescent tubes are the ideal beginner's choice.

Left: Maintaining a stable temperature is essential. A combined electronic heater/thermostat inside the aquarium gives you control over the aquatic environment at all times. Even in a centrally heated house, the ambient temperature will drop overnight. Set the heaterstat to about 18°C (64°F) as a safe minimum level.

Above: Place large and small pieces of rock onto the substrate. In nature, they would be part-buried and this is the effect we are aiming to duplicate.

Above: Start by adding water from a clean plastic measuring jug onto a flat rock or a saucer. This avoids disturbing the prewashed substrate.

Aquarium furniture and plants

Before filling the aquarium with water, it is a good idea to install any ornaments, large stones or other aquarium decor, as it is easier to move these items around at this stage. Use a clean jug to add the water, pouring it over a smooth surface, such as a large stone, so that you do not disturb the gravel. If you intend to use real plants, add water until the aquarium is only one-third to a half full. You can then put in the plants without causing an overflow. Fill the aquarium once you have added the plants

Now switch on the pumps and lights, and allow the tank to run for at least a week before adding any goldfish. This allows time for the water to reach a suitable temperature and enables you to ensure that the pumps and lights are working properly. If the tank has been planted up, it gives the plants a chance to become established before the goldfish start to nibble tender new shoots! The tank shown here features plastic plants — a safe option.

Stocking the aquarium

The recommended stocking level for a goldfish aquarium is 60cm² of water surface area for each 1cm of fish length, excluding the tail. Thus, an aquarium measuring 60 x 30 x 30cm has a surface area of 1800cm² and this divided by 60cm² means that it can hold a total of about 30cm of fish. (A 24 x 12 x 12in tank can hold 12in of fish.) This stocking level means that the fish will not be too crowded or compete for essential resources such as dissolved oxygen and food. Nor would the filtration system be adversely affected, which would result in poor water quality. We could either add twelve fish of 2.5cm (1in) and as they grow, remove some to other tanks, or have two 15cm (6in) goldfish. In any case, it is vital not to exceed the stocking capacity for the aquarium size.

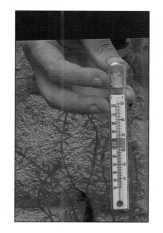

Below: Secure an internal thermometer in a top front corner of the tank, away from the current of the external power filter.

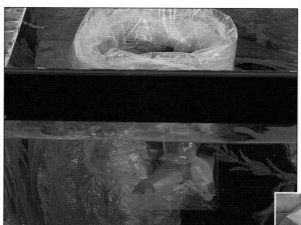

Left: Open the bag and roll down the sides to form a collar. Float the bag in the tank to equalise the water temperatures.

Below: Turn the bag on its side and hold it open with one hand while you gently tip it with the other.

Below: Leave the fish to settle for 30 minutes before turning on the aquarium lights. They will probably hide away until they feel more confident. Do not tempt them out with food.

Add fish gradually

Do not buy all your goldfish at once. It is much better to buy just two or three goldfish to start with, and providing there is no deterioration in water quality, you can add more after two or three weeks.

BUILDING A GOLDFISH POND

Whilst an aquarium is suitable for the delicate varieties of goldfish, the more robust types, such as the commons, comets and shubunkins, can be kept in an outdoor pond. Various water containers have been employed in the garden as homes for goldfish, including water butts, china sinks, water features and large ponds. However, it is worth remembering that although the goldfish you buy are usually quite small, they will grow and, after a few years, probably breed. Small containers or water features are not really suitable in the long term, as common goldfish can grow to about 30cm (12in).

When planning a goldfish pond, try to ensure that it will have a minimum surface area of about $1m^2$ (10.5 ft²) and be at least 45cm (18in) deep. If you can make it bigger, then so much the better. In the cold winter months, the goldfish will seek refuge in the deepest part of the pond, where the water is warmest. Shelves and margins are a good idea, as the shallower water will warm up quickly in the summer and provide a good area for the fish to spawn.

Siting the pond

It is important to take into account the ideal site for the pond, so that it complements the garden. It is better to use aquatic plants to provide shade for the goldfish, rather than site a pond beneath trees. If the trees are flowering species, the pond can become covered with petals in spring, and these must be removed before they sink to the bottom and decay, leading to pollution problems. Similarly, leaf fall in autumn can affect water quality and clarity by

Choosing a sunny spot

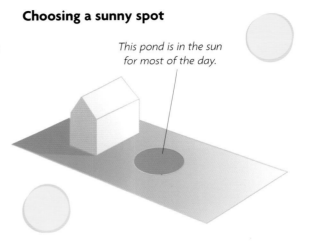

This pond is in the sun for most of the day.

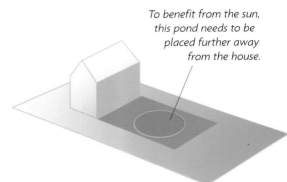

To benefit from the sun, this pond needs to be placed further away from the house.

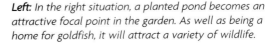

Left: *In the right situation, a planted pond becomes an attractive focal point in the garden. As well as being a home for goldfish, it will attract a variety of wildlife.*

releasing tannins into the water that stain it brown. Furthermore, the roots of trees can also cause problems, puncturing liners and even cracking concrete-lined ponds.

When choosing a site, bear in mind that the pond will need a biological filter to remove goldfish waste. Most filters are quite bulky and people generally prefer to site them behind shrubs, bamboo or some other type of screen at one side of the garden, but in a spot that allows easy access to the filter. If you cannot reach the filter easily, you may be tempted to neglect essential maintenance work, leading to a deterioration in water quality. You may also damage the pump because the water flow through it is restricted as the pump strainer and the main filter become increasingly blocked,

Pond building materials

The next point to consider is what material to use to construct the pond. Preformed glassfibre or thick plastic ponds are a popular choice. These are usually about 45-60cm (18-24in) deep, with shelves at one or two levels. They make quite robust ponds, but you will need to dig out a shape that more or less matches the moulding, otherwise the pond will not be supported correctly and the weight of the water could crack the glassfibre or plastic. These ponds are usually supplied with comprehensive installation directions, which you should follow carefully.

Pond liners made from PVC sheeting, other plastic formulations or butyl rubber are proving increasingly popular. Over the years, the manufacture of plastic and rubber materials has improved significantly. Today, the average lifespan of PVC liners is between 15 and 20 years and most butyl liners will last 30 to 40 years. Some rubber liners have a life expectancy of 80 years! Certain factors significantly reduce the

Below: Glass-reinforced plastic (GRP) is an excellent material for pond shells. It is sturdy, weather resistant and can be moulded to any shape or depth. Shells are a convenient way of creating a pond. Move them around the garden until you find the best position.

Right: Butyl rubber (top layer) is a strong, flexible, pond liner material. Newer mixes of PVC (lower layer) are just as flexible, and strong and lighter. Always choose the best quality material you can afford and buy enough for the whole excavation.

GRP shells are available in a wide range of shapes and sizes. This green colour provides an alternative to the more usual black.

Rigid plastic shells are ideal for most ponds.

Right: Pond shells made of this thick plastic are fine for a wide range of projects. They are strong, long lasting and deep enough for fish to thrive all year. Large shells of any material may be difficult to transport. Arrange delivery if necessary.

BUILDING A GOLDFISH POND

lifespan of a liner. These include creases in the fabric, which cause it to become stretched and taut, so that it loses its strength and breaks down. Another factor is exposure to air and light, both of which destabilise the structure of both PVC and butyl rubber. Usually, it is only the edges of the liner around the top of the pond that may be exposed, so the answer is to conceal the liner by 'sandwiching' it in brickwork, paving or, for a more natural look, beneath turf.

In recent years, a new liner has become available. It, too, is made of butyl, but with an added substance known as 'xavan' (pronounced 'zayvan')

sandwiched into the layers of rubber. The xavan gives the liner unique properties in that if the material is punctured, the xavan forms a seal in the hole. It means that planting baskets can be nailed in place, without any loss of water. While small holes are readily sealed by the xavan in this type of liner, regrettably, large punctures will still allow water to seep out of the pond.

Finally, there is the option of a concrete-rendered block-built pond. These can be lined with fibreglass matting or coated with coloured sealants to finish off the internal surface.

External box filter

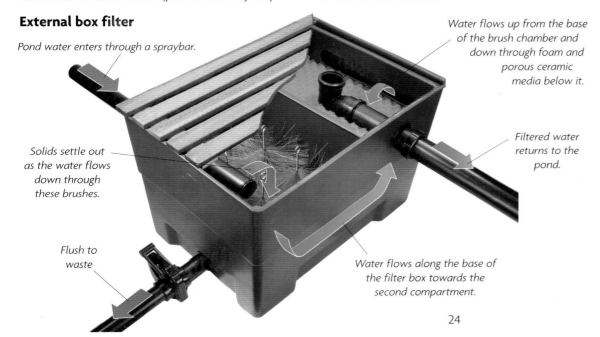

Pond water enters through a spraybar.

Solids settle out as the water flows down through these brushes.

Flush to waste

Water flows up from the base of the brush chamber and down through foam and porous ceramic media below it.

Filtered water returns to the pond.

Water flows along the base of the filter box towards the second compartment.

Safety first

Children are inevitably attracted to any pond and it is important to make the area as safe as possible for them. The most obvious deterrent is to fence off the pond, but it is easy for a child to climb over a low fence or open an access gate, so incorporate a number of safety features. Ready-made grids are now available in a range of sizes and these can be placed over the pond. Alternatively, you could approach a local blacksmith to design and manufacture an ornate, wrought-iron cover. Another option is to extend the edge of the pond with a small trench that can be filled with gravel, and plant it with tall, dense-leaved, marginal aquatic plants. The plants act as a barrier and most children will stop if their feet become wet in the gravel.

Pond filters

Although aquatic plants are very efficient at utilising the nitrogenous waste produced by goldfish, once the fish have begun to grow and breed, the plants may not be able to cope with the increased load. It is therefore a good idea to install a filter when building the pond. The filter should have two separate stages: the first, mechanical stage removes solid waste and other debris from the water, and the second, biological stage provides a substrate for beneficial bacteria and other micro-organisms to colonise. The mechanical filtration often consists of sheets of open-cell foam and these can be regularly cleaned to remove the solids and allow the water to flow through them easily. In some of the larger filters, the mechanical stage consists of a group of vertically arranged brushes. The biological part of the filter can be filled with a wide range of media, including pieces of porous ceramic material or a cartridge made up from sheets of polyester matting. It is a good idea to use water from the pond to clean the filter media. Tapwater could harm the colonies of beneficial bacteria that will build up in both parts of the filter and reduce its efficiency.

Choosing the right filter

Choose a filter system that can cope with the volume of water in your pond. Your aquatic dealer can advise you on the suitability of various models.

The filter should run continuously throughout the year. In winter, the pump can be raised from the bottom of the pond to just below the surface. (This prevents warmer deep water mixing with colder surface water and cooling the whole pond.) The pump motor relies on the surrounding water to keep it cool, and together with the running water, helps to prevent the surface of the pond from freezing over.

Some filters are fitted with an ultraviolet (UV) light unit that helps to control the microscopic algae that cause green water. The high-energy light given out by the UV tube disrupts the individual algal cells and kills them. They are then strained out by the mechanical filter medium. The UV tube is housed inside a quartz sleeve that prevents the bulb coming into contact with the water flowing past it. Be sure to clean this sleeve to remove any slime or limescale that builds up, otherwise the UV light will be diffused and the unit will not work efficiently. Do not look at the UV lamp without suitable eye protection and replace the tube every year.

Ultraviolet light units can be fitted separately from the biological filtration system. If the unit is to be sited outside, it is important to buy one of the weatherproof types.

The filter strainer excludes large particles that could block the pump impeller.

Pumps

The size of pump you will need to run your filter is usually determined by the volume of water in the pond. Ideally, the entire volume of water should pass through the filter every two hours. If the pond has a waterfall, you should fit a bigger pump to take the height, or 'head', into account. Pump manufacturers give the specifications of the head and flow rate for

Submersible pump

The pump should be easy to disassemble for cleaning.

These filter foams prevent smaller particles of debris passing through.

Choose the right size pump for the pond and make sure it is compatible with the filter.

Right: *When installing a pump, always use the largest pipe recommended and fit it directly to the pump; remember that extra fittings will slow down the flow of water.*

the pump, but if you are unsure, check with your retailer. If there are water features such as fountains or ornaments, it is better to operate these from a separate pump. This allows you to switch off the water features when they are not needed, but keep the filter running.

BUILDING A GOLDFISH POND

Establishing the goldfish pond

As soon as the pond is filled with water and the filter and any aeration systems fitted, most of us want to rush to the nearest aquatic retailer to buy our first goldfish, but it is better to wait just a little longer and start by adding the aquatic and marginal plants. Most of the pond plants on sale are quite small and usually have plenty of new shoots, which are a great temptation for goldfish to eat. It is better to start stocking the pond by adding the plants, turning on the filter system and giving them two or three weeks to become established before adding any goldfish.

Running the pond filter for a few weeks before adding the goldfish has another important effect, which is to allow any chlorine or chloramines in the tapwater to break down. Aerating the water also

Keep a separate container for mixing chemical treatments. Follow the manufacturer's directions exactly.

Left: When using algae and other treatments, prevent overdosing by first mixing them in a watering can. Then distribute them evenly around the pond.

helps to break down chloramine and vent off chlorine gas. These disinfectants are routinely added to tapwater to kill bacteria that are harmful to people, but they are poisonous to fish.

If you prefer not to have any aquatic plants and wish to stock the pond with goldfish as soon as it is completed, it vital to add a tapwater conditioner to the water to neutralise the chlorine, chloramine and other harmful tapwater additives.

The role of plants in the pond

As well as looking attractive, pond plants are very effective at removing chlorine compounds from the water and processing the waste produced by goldfish, particularly phosphate, a derivative of organic waste, and nitrate, which is the end product of the bacterial breakdown of ammonia in the biological filter. Both nitrate and phosphate are excellent nutrients for promoting plant growth, but in new ponds, these substances also encourage the growth of nuisance algae, such as green water or blanketweed. In a planted pond, the submerged and marginal species help to control nuisance algae, although it is important to realise that planting is a long-term solution and it may take several years for the plants to become fully established.

Other methods of controlling algae

While you are waiting for plants to become established, there are various chemicals that you can add to the pond water to control algae. Most of these chemicals can be very harmful to fish in soft water, so it is worth testing the carbonate hardness.

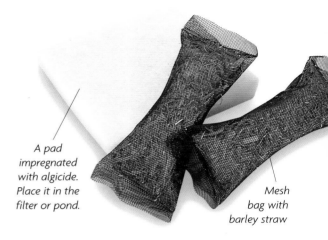

A pad impregnated with algicide. Place it in the filter or pond.

Mesh bag with barley straw

Ideally, the carbonate hardness must exceed 5°dH or 100 mg of calcium carbonate per litre in order to prevent any of the algae treatments from affecting the goldfish. Sometimes, pond water becomes soft and loses its carbonate hardness through lack of water changes. If the tapwater in your area is hard (causing limescale to form in your kettle) you can increase the carbonate hardness of the pond by making a partial water change using tapwater. In soft tapwater areas, you can raise the carbonate hardness by adding oyster shell, crushed marble or one of the proprietary chalk products to the pond before treatment with an algicide.

An organic means of controlling algae is to add barley straw, at the recommended rate of 50gm (about 2oz) per 1,000 litres (220 gallons) of pond water. The barley straw decomposes as a result of

Electronic blanketweed controller

Electronic circuitry in a sealed unit generates pulses of random electrical frequencies.

This unit is for use outside the pond.

Power lead

Treated water passes to UV steriliser if present.

Aerial lead wrapped around pipe transmits pulses into the water flow.

Pond water after passing through the main filter system.

Water after passing through blanketweed controller.

Right: Before using any chemical remedy against blanketweed, remove large algae growths with a stick to help prevent water quality problems caused by blanketweed dying in the pond.

Protecting your fish

Be aware that shelves and margins around the pond create an ideal platform for herons to catch unwary goldfish. Unfortunately, once these predatory birds have discovered a pond they can fish, they will return repeatedly, often until there are no fish left. You can protect the shallow areas by growing species of marginal plant that grow both large and dense, such as sweet flag (Acorus *sp.*), iris, rushes, lobelia or even Gunnera manicata, *which is like a giant prickly rhubarb! Usually, herons prefer to catch the fish by standing at the edge of the pond or in the shallow areas, waiting for the goldfish to swim close enough so that they can snatch them from the water with their elongated beaks. A dense planting of marginals denies the herons access to these preferred areas. There is no reason why shallow margins of the pond cannot be protected and yet still look attractive; planting is probably a better alternative to unsightly wires and nets surrounding the pond.

Below: Herons will easily spot your goldfish and in summer will catch them between and 3 and 4am.

Above: Cats are opportunistic predators, often causing nasty scratch wounds on goldfish as they try to escape the sharp claws. Cats are not natural 'fish-killers', but can be hard to dissuade once they have the 'taste'.

Left: Marginal plants such as this yellow flag iris (Iris pseudacorus) *can be used to create a dense 'wall' of vegetation around the pond to keep off cats and herons.*

the action of microscopic fungi and bacteria, which release a chemical that stops algae growing. However, the fungi and bacteria will only thrive in well-oxygenated water, so the barley straw needs to be well separated; a thick bundle will simply decay, causing the water quality to deteriorate. The chemical produced by barley straw has no effect on marginal and submerged plant species, which continue to thrive on the nutrients in the water.

Water lilies

In the past, water lilies have been traditionally associated with goldfish ponds and most certainly they can be very important for providing shade in hot weather and protection from predators such as herons. Attractively coloured varieties are now readily available, but many have quite specific requirements regarding planting depth. 'Water depth' refers to the distance of the crown to the surface and does not take into account the layer of soil in the planter. As a rule of thumb, it is usual to plant one lily for each 2.4m² (25ft²) of pond water surface.

Oxygenating plants

Oxygenating plants are considered important for providing shelter and cover in most goldfish ponds, but they are no substitute for aerating the water. Oxygenating plants have probably earned this name because it is possible to see tiny bubbles of oxygen gas on the tips of the leaves. During the day, plants photosynthesise, converting the carbon from carbon dioxide and the hydrogen and oxygen from water into sugars, using the energy of sunlight. Oxygen gas

Right: On bright, sunny days, goldfish will welcome the shade provided by water lilies and other floating plants. Their shade also helps to maintain water quality, since algae is less likely to thrive in low-light conditions.

Below: Floating plants, such as water lilies, are important in new ponds because they provide shade until the marginals have developed. Do not allow them to cover the pond completely.

is produced as a waste product and can be seen as bubbles on the leaves. At night, photosynthesis stops but respiration continues, which means that plants consume oxygen and produce carbon dioxide as waste. As long as the submerged plant growth is not too prolific, the production and consumption of oxygen is fairly stable; too many plants can deplete the oxygen, leading to mortalities among the goldfish, usually overnight.

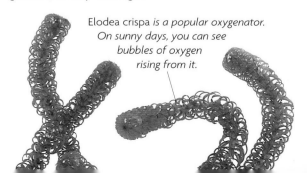

Elodea crispa is a popular oxygenator. On sunny days, you can see bubbles of oxygen rising from it.

Above: Trapa natans *grows quickly in warm weather. Remove excess plants when they cover the water surface. It is not frost hardy, so remove it from the pond in winter.*

Above: *Both azolla (tiny plants) and myriophyllum grow quickly and can take over a pond if left unchecked. Thin them at regular intervals during the growing season.*

Right: *Although not free-flowering when young,* Butomus umbellatus *(flowering rush) is worth waiting for, as the pink flowers, offset by dark green foliage, last a long time.*

Protecting the environment

A few species of exotic submerged plant have escaped from the garden pond into natural ponds and waterways, where they have become extremely invasive and damaging to the environment by out competing and killing native species of plant. These exotics include Azolla filiculoides *(water or fairy fern);* Myriophyllum aquaticum *(parrot's feather);* Hydrocotyle ranunculoides *(floating pennywort);* Crassula helmsii *(Australian swamp stonecrop) and even the familiar* Elodea canadensis *(Canadian pondweed). Instead, you could consider the many native species of really attractive oxygenating plants, including* Hottonia palustris *(water violet), with its pretty pale purple flowers;* Callitriche verna *(water starwort), which has delicate little white flowers;* Hippurus vulgaris *(mare's tail) and* Potamogeton *species, to name but a few. It is still possible for any of these oxygenating plants to proliferate in the pond and eventually become a nuisance. Probably the best way to contain them is to plant them into baskets and cut them back on a regular basis.*

Above: *Plant oxygenators in baskets covered with gravel. Lower them carefully to the bottom of the pond and allow the stems to grow to the surface.*

Right: *Pot up pond plants in aquatic soil. Add a 2.5cm (1in) layer of gravel to prevent fish disturbing them. Water the baskets before placing them on the pond shelves.*

The ideal number of oxygenating or submerged plants is 15 per 1.5m² (16ft²) of pond surface area. The best time to plant up the pond is in early summer, when a wonderful range of aquatic plants is available. This allows the plants to grow and become established during the summer months.

Buying goldfish

With the pond up and running and the plants in place, you can finally think about adding the fish. Selecting your first goldfish for the pond is an exciting occasion. Choose a reliable aquatic outlet and once there, look for plump goldfish that are active and interested in their surroundings, all indications that they are fit and healthy. Sometimes, it is a great temptation to buy the little fellow or the one with only one eye or some other obvious problem because you feel sorry for it. However, these are weak fish and the stress of netting and transporting them to their new home can be too much and they quickly get sick and die.

Introducing the fish

Having set up a new pond, it is an exciting moment when you introduce the first goldfish. Before going to buy any goldfish it is a good idea to work out just how many the pond can hold. The stocking level of a pond differs slightly from that in the aquarium, as it is the weight of fish that is used in the calculation. Generally speaking, an established pond can hold 2kg (4.4 lb) of fish per 1,000 litres (220 gallons) of water. This stocking level will allow for the goldfish to grow and later breed, so the numbers will

Left: When buying goldfish, look for alert, active fish with strong colours. Take your time to look at all the fish before deciding which ones you want.

Above: When you have made your selection, the dealer will use a large soft net to isolate the fish and then gently scoop it up in the hand and transfer it to a plastic bag that will be sealed with plenty of air or oxygen above the water.

Estimating the weight of fish

Fish length (excluding tail)		Fish weight (approx)	
cm	in	gm	oz
10-15	4-6	100-300	3.5-10.5
15-20	6-8	300-400	10.5-14.0
25-30	10-12	800-1000	28.0-35.0

Left: Take your fish home as soon as you can. The dealer will put them in a plastic bag, with air (or oxygen for long journeys) taking up most of the space in the bag. Keep it cool and in a box or covered, as fish are less stressed in the dark.

increase. It is better to buy just a few goldfish and monitor the water conditions over the next few weeks, then add a few more fish until you have reached the optimum stocking level. Between each addition of fish and before adding any more stock, it is a good idea to test the water and ensure that it is free of ammonia and nitrite. This allows the filter to mature, but without causing the water quality to deteriorate.

On reaching home, some people prefer to float the unopened bag containing the goldfish, in the pond to allow the water temperatures to equalise. This is not really a good idea for the fish because

Right: Once the goldfish have been released from the bag, they will probably swim towards the nearest plants or other shelter before venturing out to explore the pond.

even pale sunlight could cause the water inside the sealed bag to heat up very quickly and could kill the fish.

Some people believe that the best way to introduce the goldfish is to mix a little water from the pond with that in the bag to allow them to adjust to the new water. In fact, it takes the fish several days to adjust to the water conditions, so it is better to release them straightaway. Carefully open the bag and, holding the top open, gently encourage the fish to swim out by raising the bottom end.

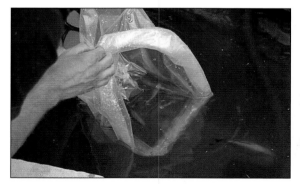

Above: Slowly tip the fish and water out into the pond, making sure all the fish are out of the bag. The fish will hide for a day or two, so there is no need to feed them. After this, feed them once a day at first, then twice a day.

FEEDING GOLDFISH

One of the most enjoyable aspects of keeping goldfish is feeding them. In addition, feeding is an important aspect of managing the goldfish and aquarium or pond. Aquarium goldfish should feed throughout the year, as the water temperature will be fairly constant. Goldfish in the garden pond will feed voraciously in the summer, but as the autumn approaches they will eat less, and in the winter, when the water temperature is very low (below 8°C/46°F), they stop feeding altogether.

Commercial goldfish food

In the wild, goldfish enjoy an omnivorous diet, meaning they eat a variety of items, including bacteria from the sediments, microscopic animals and plants, plus larger aquatic plants, insects and crustaceans. Captive goldfish should be given commercially manufactured foods that contain all the essential nutrients and vitamins to keep them fit and healthy. Flake foods are probably the most common type of manufactured diet given to goldfish, but you can also buy pellets and foodsticks for larger fish. Always gauge the size of food you offer your stock on the basis of the smallest fish to ensure that they all get sufficient to eat.

Fancy varieties of goldfish can suffer from buoyancy disorders (see page 39), and floating foods, which are consumed at the water surface, can aggravate the condition. When feeding fancy goldfish it can help if you hold the food just below the water surface and allow it to soften a little before releasing it so that it sinks, rather than floats. This prevents the fish from gulping air in addition to food.

How much to feed

One of the most commonly asked questions is 'how much food is enough?' It is generally accepted that you should offer as much food as the goldfish will eat in two or three minutes. If there is any food left over after this time, reduce the amount of feed on the next occasion. It is important not to leave any

Right: These aquarium goldfish have just been fed and are rising to the surface to eat the flakes. Goldfish are enthusiastic feeders.

Food sticks are suitable for ponds stocked with goldfish of a large size. Make sure that smaller fish do not miss out at feeding time.

Additives enhance the red colours of goldfish.

Pellets are ideal for fish too large for flake foods.

Flakes can be crumbled to suit small fish.

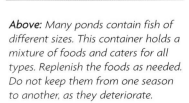

Above: Many ponds contain fish of different sizes. This container holds a mixture of foods and caters for all types. Replenish the foods as needed. Do not keep them from one season to another, as they deteriorate.

Pond feeding strategy

In the pond, the seasons and water temperatures affect feeding strategy. In the spring, as the water temperature reaches about 10°C (50°F), it is best to feed goldfish very sparingly, only giving more food if the small amount offered is consumed within a minute or so. If the food is uneaten, remove it from the pond and refrain from feeding for the next few days. At this time of the year, a single daily feed is adequate for the fishes' needs.

As the water temperature increases through late spring, the goldfish should begin to feed more actively and you can increase the amount of food you offer – but still only once a day. Once the temperature of the pond is consistently above about 16°C (61°F), feed the fish up to twice a day, and as the summer progresses, increase this to three or four times daily.

As the water temperature begins to drop with the onset of autumn, reduce the frequency of feeding, until by late autumn you are offering them food just once a day. When the water temperature drops to about 10°C (50°F) and below through the winter, the goldfish will cease feeding. Stop offering them food until the following spring.

Right: *In summer, pond goldfish feed actively on dried foods, plus insect larvae and even tadpoles.*

uneaten food in the aquarium or pond as it will decay and pollute the water. In the aquarium, one daily feed should be sufficient, but the frequency of feeding goldfish in the garden pond is dependent on the water temperature. When the goldfish first begin to feed in spring, one meal a day is adequate, but as the temperature approaches 16°C (61°F) in summer, they will feed two or three times a day.

The summer is a very important time for goldfish kept outdoors, as they must consume enough food to grow and breed, as well as store adequate reserves so that they can survive the winter when they do not feed. With the onset of autumn, reduce the frequency of feeding to just once daily.

In the past, it was assumed that goldfish in a garden pond did not need feeding as they would consume natural, aquatic life. There are two reasons why this is not acceptable. Firstly, over the last 100 years the majority of natural ponds have been lost to urbanisation, building and road construction, which has caused populations of aquatic wildlife, notably the common frog, damselfly and dragonfly, to plummet. Certainly, tadpoles and the larvae of insects, such as damselflies and dragonflies, are good eating for hungry goldfish, but feeding them on commercial diets reduces the amount of predation. The second reason is that since most ponds are more heavily stocked than they would be in the wild, the amount of food available is restricted. Competition for food is therefore intense and this can lead to stress and outbreaks of disease.

Aquarium feeding strategy

In the aquarium, it is best to feed goldfish a pinch at a time, offering them as much as they will eat in two or three minutes on a daily basis. Initially, healthy goldfish are very keen to feed and will greedily eat the food being offered. As they consume it, however, they will gradually become less active and this is the point at which to stop feeding. This will avoid overfeeding and the problems of polluting the aquarium.

Some owners prefer to soak pellet foods before offering them to their goldfish. This not only softens the food, but also stops it from floating on the surface. Fancy varieties may suffer from swimbladder disorders (see page 39) and soaking the food may help to reduce the likelihood of this happening because the food is softer and the fish do not need to gape at the surface to feed. Avoid soaking the food for more than about a minute, otherwise water-soluble vitamins such as ascorbic acid (vitamin C) will begin to leach out. Some kinds of food are not suitable for soaking in water and will disintegrate.

FEEDING GOLDFISH

Holiday feeding

Another cause for concern is what to do about feeding your goldfish while you are on a holiday. There are various ways of tackling this problem. One method is to buy 'vacation blocks', which contain food in a type of chalky block that gradually dissolves, allowing the fish to eat the feed it contains. Alternatively, during the two weeks leading up to your holiday, gradually reduce the amount of food you offer the fish until on the day of departure you stop feeding them altogether. On your return, gradually start feeding the goldfish again, so that after ten to fourteen days they are consuming their normal quantity of food.

Many people prefer to ask a neighbour or friend to look after the aquarium or pond in their absence, but if this person is not used to keeping fish, they can easily overfeed them, resulting in a build-up of water quality problems.

It is always a good idea to ask someone to check the aquarium or pond in your absence to ensure that pumps are running, so one

solution is to measure out the daily food ration into individual plastic bags and simply arrange for one portion to be given daily to the goldfish. Although pond fish may feed several times each day in the warmer weather, a single feed will suffice until you return home.

Treat foods

In addition to proprietary diets, goldfish appreciate the occasional treat food. Manufactured treat foods are available in a tablet form. The tablets adhere to the sides of the aquarium and are much enjoyed by the goldfish. Natural foods are always popular and very good for getting adult goldfish into breeding condition. Frozen foods, such as bloodworm, chopped mussels and brineshrimp, are suitable and the goldfish will relish them, but always thaw them

Below: Daphnia are microscopic creatures found in the pond, where goldfish will naturally feed on them. You can also buy stocks from aquatic outlets. Daphnia are a good first food for newly hatched fry.

A slightly different type of holiday food, but it also releases feed over a period of days.

These feeding blocks are designed to release the food over a weekend. Larger blocks last for a week or more.

Left: Bloodworms are actually insect larvae and goldfish will relish them as part of their diet. As well as frozen, they are available in freeze-dried form from aquatic stores.

out first. Like any frozen food, once it has thawed, give it to the fish straightaway. Live foods used to be considered unsuitable because of the potential risk of accidentally infecting the goldfish with parasites such as tapeworms. However, these foods are now cultured for the aquatic industry and are free of any harmful parasites.

Goldfish can also be offered lettuce. In the aquarium, you can 'plant' a leaf into the gravel or secure some in a clip attached to the aquarium glass for the goldfish to browse on. Pieces of shredded lettuce can be put directly into the pond, but remove any that are not eaten. Sometimes, lettuce can taste quite bitter, so the fish may prefer pieces of orange. In the pond, the peel can be left intact and the goldfish will strip away the flesh. In the aquarium, it is a good idea to offer just the orange flesh. These fresh oranges and lettuce are very good for the goldfish as they are an excellent source of vitamin C (ascorbic acid).

Storing food

Be careful when storing any manufactured feed that is kept in the dry in an airtight container. Only buy as much food as will be eaten within a few weeks of opening. It is false economy to buy in bulk, as the vitamin content of the food begins to break down once the container has been opened. After a few weeks the vitamin content is negligible and the food is thus of little nutritive value. If food becomes damp, discard it, as the moisture encourages moulds, which are poisonous to goldfish.

Above: *Goldfish will eat aquarium or pond plants, usually nibbling at the succulent new growth, but they do not cause any damage.*

Left: *Pieces of orange are an excellent treat food that provide fish with a fresh source of vitamin C. Remove uneaten food from the pond or aquarium before it pollutes the water.*

Left: *Lettuce is another good source of vitamins. Ideally, shred it into small pieces and allow these to float on the water surface for the goldfish to feed on. You can also buy clips to anchor individual leaves in the aquarium where the fish can graze on them.*

Keeping goldfish, whether in the garden pond or fancy varieties in an aquarium, is a very rewarding and pleasurable hobby, but as with any other pet animals, there are occasions when they become sick and we want to do our best to help them recover. The importance of good water quality has been discussed on pages 14-15, and it is vital that if a goldfish becomes sick or even dies, you should test the water to eliminate poor water quality as the cause of the problem. It is sad to realise that the commonest reasons for goldfish to become sick are attributable to inadequate management, resulting in bad water conditions. As a consequence, the fish become stressed and prone to any number of secondary diseases.

Water changes

Regular partial water changes are an important aspect of managing both the aquarium and the pond. They help to freshen the water and add salts and minerals essential to both the goldfish and plants, but always be sure to use a water conditioner to remove any chlorine from the tapwater. To prevent any health problems caused by thermal shock, always make sure that the 'new' water is at the same temperature as the pond or aquarium.

Keeping a record

It is a good idea to keep a written record of the results of any water tests and to note details of water changes – how much water was changed and when. Use the book to note changes in the behaviour of any of the goldfish, as these might indicate the start of a health problem. Writing down these details will draw attention to imminent problems and hopefully, your response will be a case of prevention rather than cure. The notebook should also contain other important information, such as the volume of water contained in the aquarium or pond. This can be invaluable if at any stage you need to add a medication to the water. If any treatments are used, including tonics or even those designed to control algae, always make a note of the dose and particularly any adverse effects.

Right: The bloated body and pinecone scalation indicate that this fish is suffering from a condition known as dropsy. This photo was taken on a warm summer's day when oxygen levels were low in the pond and this large, sick fish was the first to succumb.

First signs of trouble

Healthy goldfish have a healthy appetite and feeding them is one of the most important aspects of their management. The daily routine of feeding is a good opportunity to check that they are all eating well; often, the first indication of a health problem is when one or more goldfish has a poor appetite or is no longer feeding. When goldfish are fit and healthy, they are alert and busily swim around the aquarium or pond, often picking up pieces of gravel in their mouths and then spitting them out again. In fact,

Symptoms to look for

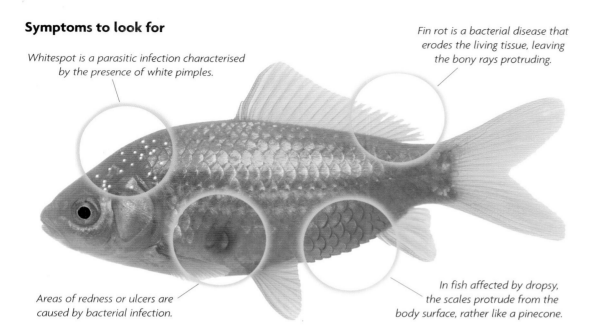

Whitespot is a parasitic infection characterised by the presence of white pimples.

Fin rot is a bacterial disease that erodes the living tissue, leaving the bony rays protruding.

Areas of redness or ulcers are caused by bacterial infection.

In fish affected by dropsy, the scales protrude from the body surface, rather like a pinecone.

they are sucking off bacteria and other microscopic life on the stones. On the other hand, sick goldfish are not very active, their fins are often clamped tightly against the sides of the body and they are usually found in the quietest part of the aquarium or pond, reluctantly moving away if disturbed.

It is worth being aware that low dissolved oxygen levels in the water will cause goldfish to become very sluggish and unwilling to feed. Increasing the amount of aeration will improve the dissolved oxygen content and if the goldfish are sick, it will help to make the environment just a little bit more comfortable for them. Another good reason for adding more air to the pond or aquarium is that if

the goldfish are unwell because the water is polluted with ammonia or nitrite, it will cause some of the pollutants to be vented off at the water surface.

The effects of stress

Stress is usually a significant factor in outbreaks of disease. Goldfish can become stressed for a variety of reasons, such as poor water conditions, bullying of fancy varieties by common goldfish, or even too much attention in the form of netting and handling. The hormones associated with stress help the goldfish to survive adverse conditions, but prolonged stress has adverse effects, particularly on the immune system, so that the fish become vulnerable

to secondary disease and infections. Diseases commonly associated with stress include whitespot and fin rot (see below).

Treating goldfish

In the event of an outbreak of disease, it is important to diagnose the problem accurately and to apply the correct medication. If you are not sure what to do, seek professional help rather than use a range of medications that may not work and could even aggravate the situation. When using any medication, be sure to follow the directions exactly and measure any treatment carefully. Never be tempted to add a few extra drops of any medication on the basis that a bit more than directed can only be helpful. Many of these treatments are very potent and even a small excess could be sufficient to overdose.

Give any treatment time to work; many medications become effective after two or three days. Never mix treatments or use a succession of different medications. Some can become highly poisonous if used in conjunction with others.

Right: When adding any treatment to aquariums or ponds, measure the dose carefully. Treatments are often supplied in containers with a built-in reservoir to ensure accurate dosing. Measure out treatments in a separate container before adding them to the pond or tank.

HEALTH CARE

Common problems

Here we look at some of the diseases that commonly affect goldfish in the aquarium or pond.

Whitespot is caused by a microscopic parasite called *Ichthyophthirius multifiliis*, probably the biggest killer of captive fish. Infected fish are lethargic, unwilling to feed and look unwell. The disease is characterised by conspicuous tiny white spots, visible over the body, fins and eyes, that look as though the goldfish is coated in white pepper. The larger white spots are the mature stage of the parasite and these rupture their way out of the skin to undergo a free-living stage, during which time they reproduce to give rise to about 2,000 infective individuals, known as

Below: The mucus on this goldfish is excessive, which can be a response to poor water conditions or a severe parasitic infection. Take action promptly.

'swarmers'. Each swarmer seeks out the goldfish and burrows beneath the skin to repeat the cycle, which in the captive environment of the aquarium or pond tips the balance very much in favour of the whitespot parasite. Treatments are effective against the free-living stage of the parasite and several are suitable for treating either the aquarium or pond.

Mature male goldfish frequently develop raised white pimples on the bony rays of the pectoral fins and around the gill cover, and these are often mistaken for whitespot. The males are usually very active, feeding and fit, and they do not appreciate being given a dose of medication, especially if it disrupts their spawning activity!

Fungus is characterised by a cottonwool-like growth on the body surface and fins of the goldfish. The fungus is actually white in colour, but usually discoloured either green or brown by dirt, detritus or even algae that gets trapped in the threads. Fungus is very invasive, penetrating deep into the muscle tissue beneath the threadlike surface, and it spreads rapidly, coating the fish within a matter of hours.

The fungal spores are found in every aquatic environment, but generally only infect a goldfish when the skin has become damaged. The damage could be the result of physical injury, such as poor handling or netting, but the integrity of the skin breaks down if the temperature drops rapidly by several degrees, or if the fish suffers from certain kinds of disease. Even poor water conditions can cause the goldfish considerable irritation, which in turn allows infections of fungus to arise. It is

Above: Outbreaks of fin rot, clearly shown here on the tail fin, are often secondary conditions. It can occur in fish affected by other diseases or in fish that are stressed by overcrowding or poor water conditions.

important to determine the reason why there has been an outbreak of fungus and rectify it, otherwise treatment will probably be ineffective.

There is a range of treatments available for controlling outbreaks of fungus, and aquarium or pond salt is excellent for treating the condition. Bear in mind that salt will affect both pond and aquarium plants, so do not use it where aquatic plants cannot first be removed easily.

Fin rot is characterised by the erosion of the delicate tissue between the bony rays of the fins, causing them to protrude, and generally the fin looks very sore at the edge where the erosion is taking place. Often the cells of the bony rays are damaged and the bones can be seen to be damaged and broken. Fin rot typically occurs when the goldfish are

stressed, be it by poor water quality, outbreaks of other disease such as whitespot or bacterial and fungal infections, or bullying by other inhabitants of the aquarium or pond. It is important to identify the underlying reason why the fish are becoming stressed in order for any medication to control the disease to be effective.

If the fin rot is very advanced, or several goldfish are affected, it may be necessary to treat the pond or aquarium with a bactericide.

Swimbladder disorders The swimbladder is a special air-filled buoyancy organ that lies in the abdominal cavity immediately beneath the spine and kidneys. The goldfish can control the amount of air in the swimbladder, filling it to rise in the water column or removing air in order to reach the bottom of the aquarium or pond. In effect, the swimbladder allows the goldfish to stay afloat at any depth in the water whilst using only a very little amount of energy.

A goldfish showing symptoms associated with swimbladder disorder either floats helplessly at the water surface or remains on the bottom of the aquarium or pond, only swimming to the surface with considerable effort. The problem seems to be especially common amongst fancy varieties of goldfish. There are several causes of the problem, which in the fancy goldfish may be associated with deformities of the swimbladder, but kidney infections, particularly those caused by certain parasite infections, may also be responsible for the condition. Unfortunately, there is no cure for a

Left: Goldfish suffering from swimbladder disorders appear to lose their balance and have difficulty staying upright. Digestive disorders, such as constipation, can also affect balance and orientation.

swimbladder disorder; sometimes, feeding seems to aggravate it, so feeding small amounts more frequently can help.

Ulcer disease is one of the commonest bacterial infections to afflict goldfish. The ulcers are visible as inflamed areas of skin, often in the form of a ring. The underlying muscle may be exposed in the centre. Goldfish that are under stress appear to be more susceptible to ulcer disease, so it is important to identify why they are suffering from this condition. If the ulcer disease is confined to just a few individuals, it may respond to treatment with an antibacterial medication. However, if a large number of fish are infected or the ulcer disease is persistent and will not heal, antibiotic medication may be required. In this case the fish will need to be examined by a veterinarian who can prescribe the appropriate treatment.

Colour loss Goldfish can lose their colour if they become sick or are exposed to poor water conditions. However, one of the commonest reasons is that the cells that produce the gold colour stop producing red pigment and the fish turns white as a result. This loss of colour can be associated with ageing in goldfish, but often it affects young fish and no doubt has a genetic origin. Although it is possible to offer the fish colour-enhancing feeds, these often do not make a great deal of difference once a goldfish has turned white.

Euthanasia

Sometimes a goldfish becomes so sick – and the swimbladder disorder described above is a case in point – that it is not going to recover and is becoming distressed. When this happens the fish usually stops feeding and fin rot ensues. At this point it is kinder to euthanase the goldfish than allow it to

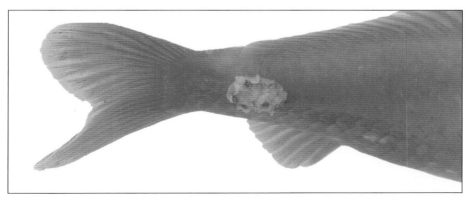

Right: A cyst or tumour is very common amongst goldfish. Although it looks unsightly, it is not infectious and will not affect others in the pond. Even the fish with the cyst can continue to function quite normally.

Above: To dispose of sick fish humanely, fill a bowl with a litre of water from the pond or aquarium and mix in the required dose of clove oil before putting in the affected goldfish.

endure a lingering death. The kindest way to do this is by using clove oil, available from most pharmacists. Mix a minimum of 10 drops of clove oil per litre of water in a suitable container before introducing the goldfish. If you feel you cannot undertake the task yourself, consult your local veterinarian.

Natural causes

Do remember that occasionally goldfish die for no apparent reason. If you have eliminated water quality as a possible cause and other fish in the pond or aquarium look fit and well, the reason may be simply old age, or even a non-infectious disease.

Quarantine strategy for aquarium goldfish

For serious goldfish hobbyists, an isolation or quarantine system is an important part of the overall setup. Keeping new fish in a quarantine system for two to three weeks does help to reduce the likelihood of introducing any infectious diseases that might rapidly affect the other goldfish. (Some hobbyists and breeders will quarantine their newly acquired fish for six months, or even more, depending on the time of the year.)

The isolation aquarium should be as large as possible and have a mature filter system. It is a common mistake to use an immature filter and as the water becomes polluted, the new fish stocks weaken and get sick, leading to the misconception that they must have been diseased when purchased. You can speed up the maturation of the filter by transplanting some filter media from another mature filter. Monitor the water quality carefully and ensure that the water temperature matches that of the main aquarium.

It is often thought that any isolation system should be used to house obviously sick fish to prevent the transfer of disease to the other goldfish. Unfortunately, in the event of an outbreak of infectious disease, which may be bacterial, viral or caused by common parasites (such as whitespot), by the time a goldfish is displaying the first symptoms of the disease, the other stock will already be infected. For outbreaks of infectious disease within an aquarium, it is better to leave the goldfish there and immediately reduce the chances of cross-infection by keeping nets separate and disinfected (using methylene blue or a povidone iodine product) and preferably drying them after use. After working on an affected aquarium, be sure to dry any splashes and wash your hands before moving on to any other aquarium.

A quarantine tank

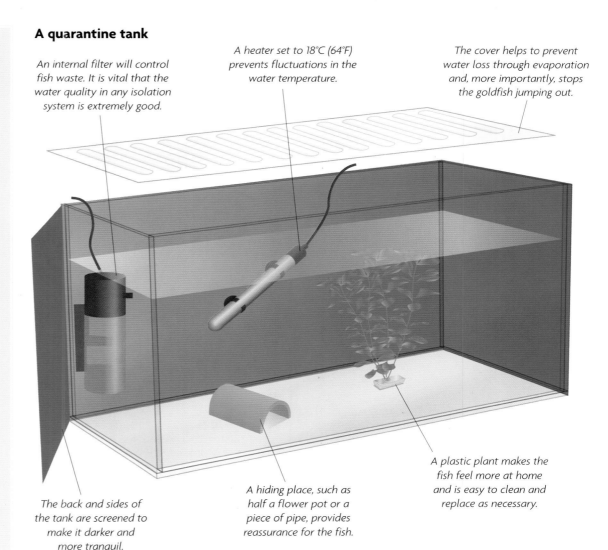

An internal filter will control fish waste. It is vital that the water quality in any isolation system is extremely good.

A heater set to 18°C (64°F) prevents fluctuations in the water temperature.

The cover helps to prevent water loss through evaporation and, more importantly, stops the goldfish jumping out.

The back and sides of the tank are screened to make it darker and more tranquil.

A hiding place, such as half a flower pot or a piece of pipe, provides reassurance for the fish.

A plastic plant makes the fish feel more at home and is easy to clean and replace as necessary.

For many people, the ultimate reward of keeping goldfish is breeding them. In the garden pond, this probably takes place more by accident than design, when the water temperature is consistently above about 16°C (61°F), but goldfish have been known to breed in ponds with a temperature as low as 10°C (50°F), providing the fish are healthy.

Differentiating between the sexes

It can be quite difficult to differentiate between the sexes of both common and fancy goldfish. Usually, the female, or 'hen', goldfish has a much rounder appearance than the male, due to the development of eggs in the paired ovaries, which lie just beneath the swimbladder on each side of the body cavity. In fancy goldfish, it is more difficult to see whether the female is plumper, as both males and females tend to have short, deep bodies.

Males, or 'cock', fish often develop tubercles – also called a spawning rash – when they are in breeding condition. These resemble raised white pimples, about the size of a pinhead, predominantly on the gill cover and bony rays of the pectoral fins. It is possible for the tubercles to be mistaken for the

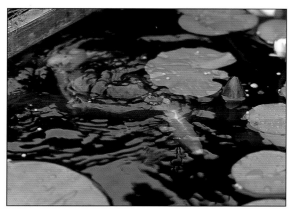

Above: It is often possible to tell that the goldfish are about to spawn because they become increasingly active, particularly amongst the aquatic plants at the margins of the pond.

Left: The spawning rash can be seen as raised white pimples on the gill covers of this male fish. These have quite an abrasive feel and the male may use them during the spawning behaviour to arouse the females.

disease whitespot (see page 38), but usually males that are ready to breed are very fit and energetic, whereas whitespot leaves fish unwell, often lethargic and lacking in appetite. Just to make it more difficult to sex goldfish, some males may never develop a spawning rash, whilst there have also been reports of females with tubercles.

Spawning

In the pond, the onset of spawning is noticeable as the goldfish become increasingly active, swimming excitedly up and down, with the males beginning to chase the females. The females seem to try to escape the attentions of the males, but are attracted towards areas of dense aquatic vegetation, which is where they will lay their eggs. When she is ready to release her eggs, a single female goldfish followed by several males swims into the aquatic vegetation. As she lays her eggs, the males swim immediately behind, shedding milt (sperm) to fertilise them. Within a few seconds of being released, the eggs will stick to the leaves of the plants, regardless of whether they are fertilised or not. Eggs that were not fertilised tend to turn a milky white colour within a few hours, whereas the embryo goldfish begin to develop in the fertile eggs.

Spawning is supposed to begin at dawn, but in reality it seems to take place when the goldfish are ready to breed, and may continue throughout the day, with the females laying between 2,000 and 4,000 eggs. If there is an abundant food source, the goldfish will spawn repeatedly through the summer. After spawning, the females are often exhausted;

Making a spawning mop

1 You can make your own spawning mops very easily. Wind green nylon wool around a piece of card or the short side of this book until you have about 30 strands. Cut off the surplus.

2 Cut another piece of wool about 20cm (8in) long from the ball and thread it under the strands. Secure the strands with a tight knot.

3 Turn over the card or book and cut the wool strands at the point opposite your knot. You now have a spawning mop. Do not cut off the long ends of the wool securing the strands.

sometimes the males have been quite rough during their courtship, leading to wounds or injuries. As a consequence of reproduction, the females' immune system is suppressed and at this time, they can be vulnerable to secondary infections.

The eggs are a good source of nutrients and will be eaten not only by other fish in the pond or aquarium, but also by the parents. This is one of the reasons why, although the goldfish spawn, there never appear to be any young fish. In order to prevent this cannibalism, it is a good idea to remove some of the plants with the eggs attached to an aquarium and rear the resulting fry until they are

4 Wash the mop in warm running water before placing it in the tank. Use the long ends of wool securing the strands to tie the mop to a cork or to suspend it from the surface of the aquarium.

2-3cm (0.8-1.2in) long. At this stage, they are less vulnerable to predation by other fish.

Hatching

The speed with which the goldfish embryo develops depends on the water temperature, and hatching can take between six and seven days at 16°C (61°F), three days at about 25°C (77°F) and just two days at 30°C (86°F). In the pond, hatching can take a few days, but in the more controlled temperatures of the aquarium (between 22 and 23°C/72-74°F), the young goldfish should hatch in four to four-and-a-half days.

The tiny goldfish larvae with large eyes that hatch from the eggs are just a few millimetres long. Immediately after hatching, the larvae feed on the remains of the yolk, but once this has been consumed, they undergo a process known as 'swim up'. The larvae swim to the water surface and take a gulp of air, which inflates the swimbladder, and at this stage they are called fry. Once the swimbladder is full of air, the fry can swim actively and must begin to feed on microscopic animals. If there is insufficient food available, they will die within a few hours, but where the food is abundant, the little fry grow rapidly.

Developing fry

On hatching, the fry are a green-brown colour, but over a period of time, in metallic fish the colour changes to black and then red. Calico fish hatch a green-brown colour, but the colours begin to develop in about two weeks. One of the problems with goldfish spawning naturally is that most have genes for brown or wild-type colour, with the result that many of the offspring remain brown or bronze, rather than developing the desired gold colour. Brown goldfish can breed to produce red goldfish, but over successive generations the numbers of brown fish increase. Some ponds may also contain a mix of goldfish varieties, such as common, comets, wakin and shubunkins, and they will interbreed, usually with disappointing results. It might be surprising to discover that goldfish will also breed with koi or ghost carp and although the young will have characteristics of both parents, this does not include colour; the babies tend to be brown.

Controlled spawning

The results of goldfish spawning naturally are unpredictable, but controlled propagation or spawning allows you to select the broodstock (parent fish) and, therefore, the production of fry with desirable colour or characteristics. Pond goldfish, which are used to a great deal of freedom, may become stressed if they are placed in an aquarium and this may stop them coming into breeding condition. Ideally, provide a tank that is as large as is practically possible. It should be equipped with a simple sponge filter, otherwise the larvae or fry will be sucked into the pump mechanism of powerhead or external filters.

Liquid fry food is a specialist diet for newly hatched fish. It contains micro-organisms in suspension. Squeeze the plastic bottle and drip the food into the tank.

The broodstock is usually selected during the summer or autumn months, in preparation for spawning the following year. In some countries, males and females are kept together in the same suitably sized aquarium, as it is thought that the presence of the female influences breeding condition in the male. When the broodstock goldfish are housed in the same aquarium, they are both treated alike with regard to feeding and given high-protein diets to condition them for breeding.

Traditionally, once the broodstock has been selected, males and females are kept in separate tanks until the goldfish breeder is ready to pair them. Spawning usually takes place within a few days, providing the fish are healthy and in good condition. The females use up a great deal of their food

A goldfish breeding tank

Right: Place two male goldfish in the breeding tank with one female. They should spawn within a few days. Once the eggs are laid, remove the parent fish to prevent them eating the eggs.

Leave the spawning mop undisturbed to allow the eggs to develop. Ideally, the water should be 15cm (6in) deep for the tiny fry, so reduce the water depth once the fish have spawned.

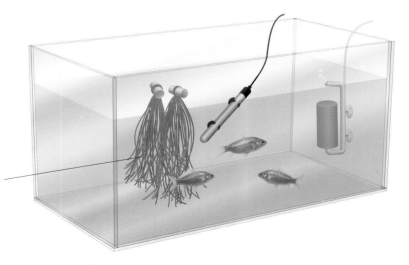

resources in producing eggs, so feed the broodstock on a good-quality, high-protein diet, supplemented with chopped earthworms, live daphnia, bloodworms, frozen tubifex or cockles. Thaw frozen foods before serving them to the fish and chop large pieces into bite-size morsels.

Eggs will be produced by the ovaries almost as soon as the female has finished spawning, and a good-quality, high-protein diet will enable her to use the nutrients to prepare for reproduction the following year. The production of sperm, or milt, by the males requires far less energy, so it is usual to commence feeding them with a high-protein diet in late winter or early spring.

By early summer, the abdomen of the females should be rounded and swollen with eggs, and in males there may be signs of a spawning rash. To ensure that spawning takes place, the water in the aquarium should ideally be held at 20°C (68°F). Regular partial water changes, undertaken as part of the management regime, may also trigger spawning. Once the fish have spawned, remove the parents to prevent them eating the eggs. If they are in peak condition and are returned to a good-quality, high-protein diet after spawning, they should remain in good condition and are likely to spawn again.

Rearing fry

It is important to ensure that the water in the aquarium with the eggs is maintained at the highest quality. The growing embryos produce a considerable amount of ammonia as waste and this pollutant is very poisonous to the growing goldfish. Monitor the water for ammonia and undertake partial water changes if necessary. It will be about two days after the goldfish fry have hatched before they need to be given any food. You can offer them proprietary liquid foods or feed them on brineshrimp cultivated in advance. Like any young animal, the fry need frequent feeding – ideally every four hours. As this may be difficult, feed the fry heavily; they will continue to hunt for the live brineshrimp. However, brineshrimp cannot live long

These nine-week-old red metallic ranchus already have a good body shape, but the hood may take three years to develop.

in freshwater and will soon die. Siphon them out of the tank to prevent the water becoming polluted.

After a couple of weeks, the diet of the fry can be supplemented with a manufactured flake diet, crumbled to a suitable size. Alternatively, mix the flake or dried food with sieved daphnia and just enough water to make a stiff dough. Feed pieces of the dough to the young fish throughout the day, but remove the remains of the previous meal each time to prevent the aquarium from becoming polluted and affecting the water quality.

Growing on

As the goldfish grow in size, their numbers will need to be thinned out by stocking them into other tanks. If there are too many in the aquarium, they will be competing for food resources, with the result that they do not achieve good growth rates. Long-finned varieties tend to grow at a slower rate, and it can be a good idea to separate the long-finned fry from the others, as this allows them to feed more easily.

A single spawning may result in at least 1,000 fry, but despite this large number, only a handful will have the characteristics required of good specimens

Three attractive young metallic veiltail-type orandas at just nine weeks old. The breeder will have selected them for growing on.

of fancy goldfish, such as colour, desirable fin and body shape. Regrettably, some of the fancy goldfish fry will require culling; even though the parents were carefully selected. The first cull is undertaken when the goldfish are about two months old and a large number will be probably be discarded. Over the next few months, it is important to continue feeding heavily, especially the deep-bodied varieties of fancy goldfish, such as ryukin and veiltail, and those with head growth, such as lionhead and ranchu. At the same time, you must ensure that the water quality is not affected.

The culling remains a continuous process for about three years, and involves selecting only the best goldfish each time. If you selected good-quality broodstock, you can expect a higher percentage of good offspring. Success in breeding fancy goldfish is not only the result of selecting good parental stock, but also in the rearing and culling of the fry.

The shape of the veiltail is already clear to see, but the hood has yet to develop.

SHOWING GOLDFISH

Successfully rearing goldfish to produce high-quality specimens with the desirable attributes for the particular variety takes dedication and patience. For serious breeders, the mark of success lies in showing fancy goldfish. Shows are not only attended by people who breed goldfish, but also by hobbyists who have acquired good-quality specimens and wish to exhibit them. The shows give them a chance to demonstrate their ability to manage and maintain the fish. Achieving the high standards of quality and condition required for showing takes a great deal of

Below: The highlight of the year for goldfish breeders is the show. These are fishes in their show tanks after judging. The labels on the tanks indicate the position achieved and points scored. When the judging is over, exhibitors and the public are allowed into the hall.

care and skill. You might think that shows are confined to the fancy varieties, but they also include common goldfish, shubunkins and comets.

All the varieties are judged by set standards in five categories, namely body, fins, colour, special characteristics, and condition and deportment. Each category has a starting figure of 20 points, making a possible total of 100, but with marks deducted for faults. In some instances, characteristics are bred into goldfish for which they may be marked down or even disqualified, as these are not incorporated into the standards for that particular variety.

Type testing goldfish

Before any goldfish entered for a show can be judged and points deducted from the possible 100, they are type tested. Type testing means that specific features required for that variety are checked to ensure they meet the standard. Once the goldfish has passed the type testing, then it will be judged against others in that variety.

The body

The symmetry of the body is very important. Quality fish are muscular, with a smooth shape and outline, and their colour or colours must be correct for the particular variety. The length and depth of the body must also conform to certain standards. The scales, although not scored as such, need to be a good, even shape and regularly arranged.

The fins

The fins should be well developed, perfectly matched and of the appropriate size for the variety. In twintail goldfish, which have paired caudal and anal fins, the fins should be identical in size and shape. All the fins should spread beautifully and there should be no folds. Where present, the dorsal fin should stand up straight; curving at the tip is unacceptable. In many varieties the dorsal fin is absent, and in these fish the back should be perfectly smooth, with no remnants of the fin or fleshy spurs present. Finally, remember that it is very easy to damage delicate fins through netting or handling and this would, of course, be marked down when showing the goldfish.

Colour

Colour is another important standard by which goldfish are judged. Metallic fish include single-coloured goldfish and those with combinations of two or more colours, which should be strong and bright. The pattern created by the colours should be even and balanced. Amongst the calico varieties of goldfish, the depth of the pigment cells gives rise to the coloration, but blue, white, red and black, and sometimes other colours, such as violet or brown, are also present. In calico fish, it is important that the reds are really bright and that the black is a sooty colour. Colour is subject to changes due to environment, age and temperature, so it is common for the colours to change, which in turn may affect the quality of any show goldfish.

Special characteristics

It is the special characteristics that are the essence of the fancy goldfish and the wide variety includes the hoods, bubble-eyes, telescope-eyes and pompons, to name but a few. In each case, the special characteristics should be prominent, because they define the varieties.

Condition and deportment

The condition of the goldfish is obviously important, as there would be little point in showing specimens with damaged scales or fins. It may seem strange to include deportment in the showing of goldfish, but of course if a specimen swims elegantly and steadily, it will display the beauty of its movement and attitude – features for which it is being judged.

You can acclimatise a show goldfish to the procedure by placing it in a show tank, so that it becomes used to being on its own and having people passing by or peering into the tank. The goldfish needs to be alert but not frightened by the unfamiliar surroundings.

The benefits of the goldfish show extend beyond the ability to display specimen fish and win prizes. Shows provide breeders with a measurement of their success in raising particular varieties of goldfish. Hobbyists seeking a pedigree strain of a certain variety of fish can see the quality produced by a particular breeder and, of course, any show is an open forum for discussion and debate on the hobby in general.

Judging a red metallic ranchu (total score: 75.5 points)

Body (20 points)	Possible	Actual
Depth & length	6	5
Dorsal contour	5	4
Ventral contour	3	1.5
Lateral contour	3	3
Eyes & mouth	3	3
	20	16.5

Special characteristics (20 points)

The special characteristic of this variety is the development of the wen (hood) in three main areas:

	Possible	Actual
Cranial region	10	8
Infra-orbital region	5	3.5
Opercular region	5	4
	20	15.5

Condition and deportment (20 points)
The deportment ha been marked low because of a tendency to hang head down.

	Possible	Actual
Condition	10	9
Deportment	10	6
	20	15

Colour (20 points)
The red of this fish is not of the highest intensity and does not extend into the fins.

Actual score: 13 points

Fins (20 points)
Assuming the fish has twin anal fins and a divided caudal, all the other fins are good but not perfect.

Actual score: 16 points

Twintailed goldfish are among the most popular varieties.

Part Two

A variety for every hobbyist

The wide choice of goldfish varieties, with their different characteristics and individual personalities, appeals to a range of hobbyists. Probably most people are familiar with the variations in the shape of the tail fin, which may be used to differentiate between varieties and place them into categories, such as singletails, twintails and other varieties. The most obvious singletailed variety must be the common goldfish and the other pond fish favourites, the comet and the London and Bristol shubunkins. Twintailed goldfish are subdivided into long- or veiltailed, and short- or fantailed, varieties. The caudal fins of both the veiltail and fantail are divided, but in the former, they are deeply divided and the fins are long and full. In the best specimens, they hang down in graceful folds. Veiltailed fish include the veiltail, oranda and moor, while the fantail, pearlscale, lionhead, celestial and bubble-eye are typical short-tailed goldfish.

In addition to the body shapes, there are variations in the colour and colour patterns amongst goldfish. The pigment cells in the skin produce three main colours – black, red and yellow. Single-coloured goldfish have a predominance of one of these types of cell. Some goldfish appear blue, because the pigment cells that produce black lie very deep within the skin tissue. Silver (white) is due to an absence of any pigment cells. Other colours are the result of a mixing of the pigments produced by the cells. Scales may also enhance the underlying colours, whether they are metallic, nacreous or matt. Shubunkins often have a large number of matt scales, which makes them appear largely scaleless.

Like most members of the carp family, all the varieties of goldfish are peaceful and will happily coexist. Although you can successfully keep different varieties of goldfish in the same aquarium, it is not always advisable. Singletailed goldfish are very active and fast moving and will often harass the slower, round-bodied, fancy varieties. It is also better to keep bubble- and telescope-eyed goldfish separately, as they cannot see particularly well and can lose out in competition for food resources. The tissue supporting the eyes is also very delicate and can be readily injured.

A good-quality common goldfish should have a body shape similar to that of its wild-type ancestors. That is, a body depth of no more than three-eighths of its body length, excluding the tail, and a gently curved dorsal profile. The length of the body should be slightly more than twice the depth and the dorsal profile gently curved. The pectoral and pelvic fins are paired and the dorsal, caudal (tail) and anal fins should be single. The caudal fin should be short and stumpy, and all the other fins should be rounded and like little paddles.

Common goldfish are metallic and can be either all one colour (self-coloured) or a combination of colours (variegated). Self-coloured common goldfish include red, orange, yellow, blue, brown, and black, which should be intense, bright and clear. Variegated common goldfish feature the above colours but also include silver in different combinations. The patterns should be balanced and clear, extending into the fins.

Although the common goldfish is probably the most popular variety, achieving a good-quality specimen of show standard is actually quite difficult.

The body should look sturdy, with a smooth outline.

The caudal peduncle should be strong and well-developed, with a short tail fin.

Above: *Without doubt, the goldfish is one of the most widely kept fish. Common goldfish are farm-reared for the general 'pet' market and keen hobbyists focus on breeding high-quality specimens, such as this red one.*

In recent years, these yellow goldfish have become very popular, often being sold as 'canary goldfish'.

Left: *Common goldfish are available in self-coloured forms, such as this elegant yellow one, or even in variegated colours.*

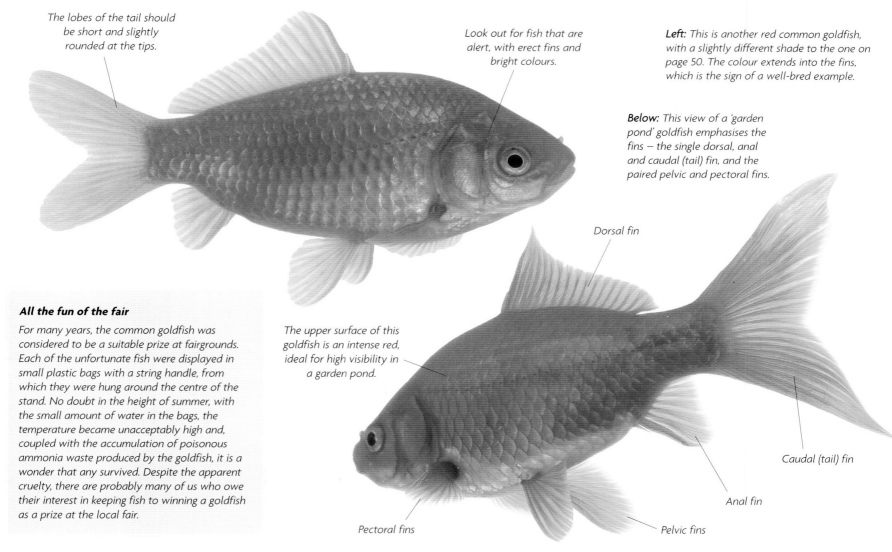

The lobes of the tail should be short and slightly rounded at the tips.

Look out for fish that are alert, with erect fins and bright colours.

Left: This is another red common goldfish, with a slightly different shade to the one on page 50. The colour extends into the fins, which is the sign of a well-bred example.

Below: This view of a 'garden pond' goldfish emphasises the fins – the single dorsal, anal and caudal (tail) fin, and the paired pelvic and pectoral fins.

Dorsal fin

The upper surface of this goldfish is an intense red, ideal for high visibility in a garden pond.

Caudal (tail) fin

Anal fin

Pectoral fins

Pelvic fins

All the fun of the fair

For many years, the common goldfish was considered to be a suitable prize at fairgrounds. Each of the unfortunate fish were displayed in small plastic bags with a string handle, from which they were hung around the centre of the stand. No doubt in the height of summer, with the small amount of water in the bags, the temperature became unacceptably high and, coupled with the accumulation of poisonous ammonia waste produced by the goldfish, it is a wonder that any survived. Despite the apparent cruelty, there are probably many of us who owe their interest in keeping fish to winning a goldfish as a prize at the local fair.

The comet has always been popular as a pond fish, particularly in the United States, where the variety is thought to have originated. The features of a good comet are like those of a first-rate common goldfish, but with a more slender body. The pectoral and pelvic fins should be paired, and the dorsal, anal and caudal fins single. Generally, the fins are longer and more elegant than those of the common goldfish, but the main difference is in the caudal fin, which is deeply forked and must be at least half (ideally three-quarters) the length of the body. The lobes of the caudal fin should be clearly pointed at the tips and held spread, without folding or overlapping. The colour should be intense and extend into the fins.

Comets may be metallic in colour or calico. The metallic specimens may be self-coloured or variegated, calicos should have at least 25% of the body colour to be blue, with the colour patches and black spots as described for the shubunkin. One of the most popular variegated colours is the sarasa comet – red and silver.

Right: *This red metallic comet clearly shows the elongated fins and long, deeply forked tail typical of the variety.*

Wakin – variation on a common theme

Once the most common variety of goldfish in Japan, the wakin appears to all intents and purposes like a common goldfish, ideally with a fanlike tail. The body is long and torpedo-shaped, all the fins except the caudal are short, and the dorsal and anal fins are single. The caudal fin is the really prominent feature, which should be divided and forked. The wakin can grow quite large, easily reaching 30cm (12in) in length. Wakins are metallic, self-coloured and variegated.

Above: A well-balanced sarasa comet with the red-and-silver patterning characteristic of this colour form. The forked tail should have well spread lobes that are straight without kinks.

Right: These young sarasa comets are very active and constantly on the move. They have a bright and shiny finish to their bodies, almost as if they have been polished. The best specimens have colour extending into the extremities of the fins.

GOLDFISH VARIETIES – SHUBUNKIN

There are two different varieties of shubunkin, the London shubunkin and the Bristol shubunkin. Both should have paired pectoral and pelvic fins, single dorsal, anal and caudal fins, and a smooth overall body shape as already described for the common goldfish. Their distinguishing feature is that they should have calico colours. In shubunkins, blue is an important colour and for show quality fish, at least 25% of the body must be of this colour. The blue should form the background colour and there should be areas of violet, red, orange, yellow and brown. Finally, there should be an even distribution of black spots. Good-quality fish have intense coloration, which extends into the fins.

Overall, the fins of the Bristol shubunkin are larger than those of the London, but the main difference is in the size and shape of the caudal fin. In Bristol shubunkins the caudal fin has semicircular, rounded lobes that almost look like the letter 'B'. As the Bristol shubunkin swims, all of the fins should be well spread and the lobes of the caudal fin should not overlap in a scissorlike action.

Below: The distinctive caudal fin with beautifully rounded lobes clearly marks this fish out as a Bristol shubunkin. All the fins are longer than on the London shubunkin.

Right: This typical London shubunkin has the body shape of a common goldfish combined with calico colours, dominated by a blue background. Colour should extend into the fins.

The body of the fantail is deep – at least three-fifths of the body length. The dorsal fin is single, and all the other fins should be paired and have slightly rounded tips. The caudal fin should be both divided and forked and is the major characteristic of the fantail. As the fish swims, the caudal fin should not drop or fold and, when viewed from above, should have a fan shape. Originally, standards were set for two different variations of the caudal fin – a longer, finer, flowing tail, or a shorter and rather stumpy tail. However, rather than keeping them separate these have been amalgamated to a single standard for the variety fantail.

Metallic self-coloured and variegated fantails should have colour of a good depth and quality, extending into the fins. Calico fantails should be mainly blue, with patches of colour similar to shubunkins, and black spots.

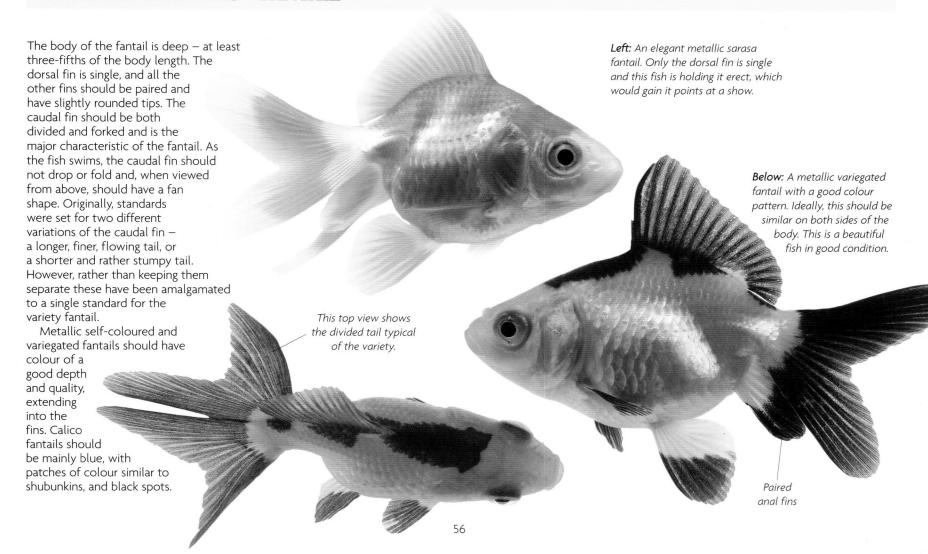

Left: An elegant metallic sarasa fantail. Only the dorsal fin is single and this fish is holding it erect, which would gain it points at a show.

Below: A metallic variegated fantail with a good colour pattern. Ideally, this should be similar on both sides of the body. This is a beautiful fish in good condition.

This top view shows the divided tail typical of the variety.

Paired anal fins

Ryukin

The ryukin is regarded as a Japanese variety of goldfish, supposedly having arrived there via the Ryukyu Islands, which lie between Japan and Taiwan. The ryukin is a very popular fish in Japan and is quite large, attaining a size of about 20cm (8in). The body is deep, with a very pronounced hump immediately behind the head, which is long and distinctly pointed in shape. The dorsal fin is high and the long tail fin may have either three or four lobes. The three-lobed tail should have a slight indentation, which is known in Japan as the 'cherry blossom petal tail'. The ryukin can be self-coloured metallic, variegated or calico.

Right: Red-and-silver ryukins such as this are regarded by the Japanese as the best examples of the variety. The pattern should be balanced and the red should be a rich deep colour, as it is here.

The dorsal fin is high and single. All the other fins are paired.

Left: A striking calico ryukin with a very good body shape. Note the steep front profile of the hump bearing the dorsal fin and the typical sharply pointed head.

Paired pelvic fins, with the paired anal fins just behind.

Single-tailed ryukin

A single-tailed variety of ryukin developed in the Yamagata Prefecture of Japan is known as the Yamagata Kingyo, Sabao or Tamasaba. Where available, it is sold as a pond fish as it is very tolerant of the cold. These fish have striking red-and-white coloration.

The veiltail has a short, deep body, which should be more than two-thirds of the body length. The dorsal fin – the only single fin – is long, its height being roughly two thirds of the body depth. The pectorals, and in particular the pelvic fins, should be long and narrow. The paired caudal fin is the prominent feature of this variety and should be flowing and long, at least three-quarters of the body length. The edge of the caudal fin should not be forked or have pointed lobes but should be divided when viewing the fish from above. As a veiltail swims, the dorsal fin should be upright and flow rather like a flag, without bending or sagging. The caudal fin should flow gracefully.

Calico or metallic self-coloured and variegated forms of veiltail are acceptable, but the colours must be strong and extend into the fins.

Although very popular, good-quality veiltails conforming to the required standard are difficult to breed. Breeding pairs of veiltails often fail to produce offspring similar to the parental variety.

Right: A red metallic veiltail with the typical high dorsal fin and long, narrow pelvic and pectoral fins. The flowing fins are easily damaged and so it is best to keep this variety with other long-finned goldfish varieties.

Left: The paired tail fin of this calico veiltail is flowing and graceful. The trailing edge of the fin is squared off, with no pointed lobes – a feature of this variety. An extensive amount of bright blue forms the background to the calico colour pattern. The red coloration on the head is a good feature. The dorsal fin is 'in tune' with the body size and the other fins.

The oranda, originally bred in Holland, has a short, deep body, roughly two-thirds of the body length. The dorsal fin should be single and high, with all other fins paired and long. The caudal fins should be divided, like that of the veiltail, and current standards call for the trailing edge of the tail to be more like the square edge of the black moor and veiltail. Orandas bred in the Far East tend to have the trailing edge of the caudal fins deeply forked. In the West, specimens of oranda with a forked tail can be shown but points will be deducted for this feature. As it swims, the fins of the oranda should flow gracefully. The main characteristic of the oranda is the development of wartlike excrescences to form a hood – technically called a wen – on the head. In good specimens, each of the little rounded excrescences should be of the same size. Recently, the Chinese have bred orandas with telescope eyes.

In addition to metallic, self-coloured, variegated and calico colour types, there is a separate category for the redcap oranda. In this variety, as the name suggests, the hood is a deep red and should be confined to the crown of the head, while the body should be silver. Among the metallic and calico varieties, the hood should cover the top of the head, extending around the eye and onto the gill covers.

Above: *Three young orandas. At this early stage you should be looking for a generous width across the head/between the eyes, making a good platform for wen (hood) development.*

Right: *Whilst the colouring of this young fish looks attractive, the black markings are only temporary and will eventually become totally red.*

The developing hood

The wartlike growth on the head – the wen, or hood – develops gradually in three areas: the top of the head, around the eyes, and around the gill covers. The tiny lumps which make it up are quite soft to the touch. Here, the emerging areas of hood are pinpointed by the white spots and filmy covering on the skin. Development can be variable and in some specimens the hood never forms.

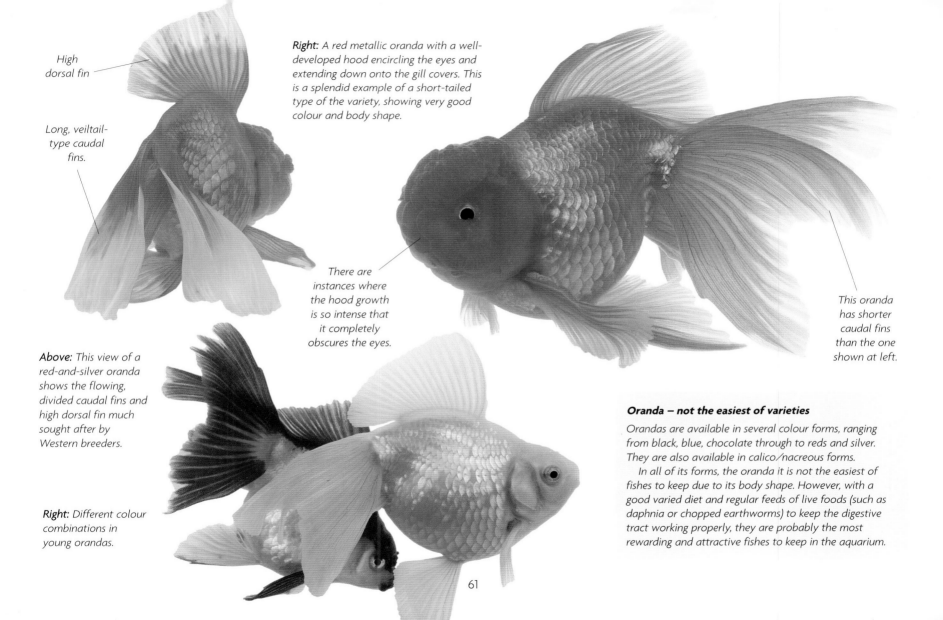

High
dorsal fin

Long, veiltail-
type caudal
fins.

Right: A red metallic oranda with a well-developed hood encircling the eyes and extending down onto the gill covers. This is a splendid example of a short-tailed type of the variety, showing very good colour and body shape.

There are instances where the hood growth is so intense that it completely obscures the eyes.

This oranda has shorter caudal fins than the one shown at left.

Above: This view of a red-and-silver oranda shows the flowing, divided caudal fins and high dorsal fin much sought after by Western breeders.

Right: Different colour combinations in young orandas.

Oranda – not the easiest of varieties

Orandas are available in several colour forms, ranging from black, blue, chocolate through to reds and silver. They are also available in calico/nacreous forms.

In all of its forms, the oranda it is not the easiest of fishes to keep due to its body shape. However, with a good varied diet and regular feeds of live foods (such as daphnia or chopped earthworms) to keep the digestive tract working properly, they are probably the most rewarding and attractive fishes to keep in the aquarium.

61

The globe-eye variety of goldfish is also known as the telescope-eye in the USA and the dragon fish in the Far East. The overall body shape is similar to that of the veiltail, with a single dorsal fin and pointed tips to the other fins, all of which should be paired. The eyes protrude from the head – hence the variety name. The caudal fin should be forked to about a quarter of its length and long – approximately three-quarters of the body length.

In good-quality specimens, the eyes should be at the tip of truncated cone-shaped protuberances and should be symmetrical. As the fish swims, the dorsal fin should be erect and the caudal fin should flow.

Metallic self-coloured and calico globe-eyes occur. The calicos must be bright and have a blue background with brown, orange, red, yellow and violet patches, spotted with black.

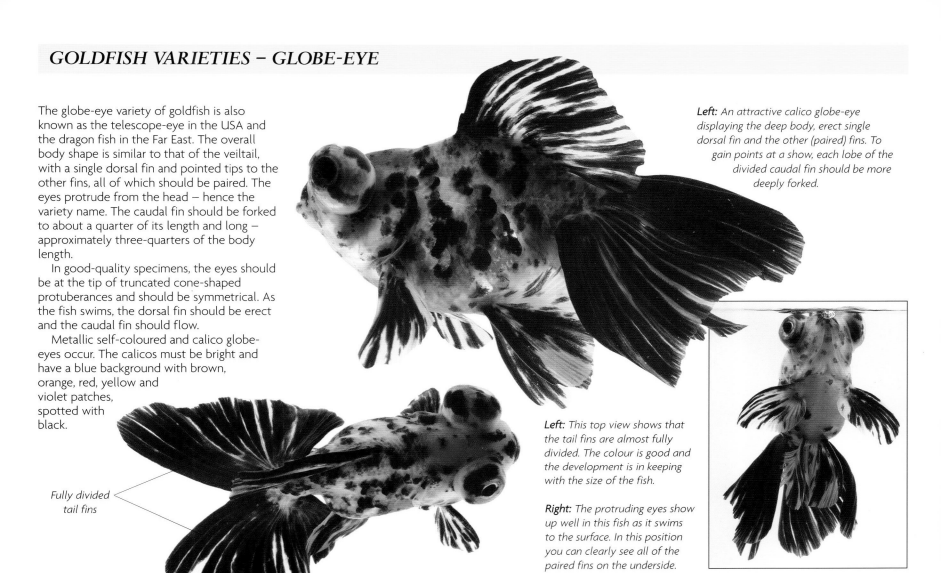

Left: An attractive calico globe-eye displaying the deep body, erect single dorsal fin and the other (paired) fins. To gain points at a show, each lobe of the divided caudal fin should be more deeply forked.

Fully divided tail fins

Left: This top view shows that the tail fins are almost fully divided. The colour is good and the development is in keeping with the size of the fish.

Right: The protruding eyes show up well in this fish as it swims to the surface. In this position you can clearly see all of the paired fins on the underside.

This fish would be an asset to the owner. Three or four fish like this in a 90cm (3ft) tank would form the perfect living picture.

Upright dorsal fin

Below: A red-and-black globe-eye in good condition, showing a high and upright dorsal fin and very good body shape. Looking at both the side and top views, this fish clearly has even markings – a good feature.

Comparing both sides reveals good, even eye development.

Left: This top view shows a well-balanced fish, with a straight back, fully divided tail and well-positioned eyes.

63

The broadtail moor may also be popularly known as the black moor. Essentially, this variety is a self-coloured black version of the veiltail, with a short, deep body. The notable difference between them is the moor's protrusive eye shape, which should be spherical overall. The dorsal fin should be high and is single, whereas all the other fins are paired. Just as in the veiltail, the caudal fin should be divided but neither forked nor with pointed lobes. The tips of the fins should be rounded. The fish should be a rich velvety black, without any brown or silver. However, in practice, the colour can be difficult to obtain; it should be a sooty, velvety black, extending right down to the belly.

Right: *The tail fin of the broadtail moor should be flowing and graceful, and the trailing edge should be more or less straight. The eyes should be large and protrude from the head, almost as if they were stuck on the surface.*

As the name implies, this variety is black and white (silver). Ideally, the colouring should be intensely black and like polished silver in a well-balanced pattern on either side of the body. The eyes are similar to those of the black moor. Another feature of this variety is the butterfly tail. When buying panda butterflies, look for bright, alert specimens, with all their fins well spread. This variety is very similar to the globe-eye.

Note the upright dorsal fin

A beautiful example of a butterfly tail, showing fully divided and equal-sized lobes.

Above: *This is a well-balanced little panda butterfly goldfish in exceptional condition and displaying well.*

Left: *The panda butterfly, sometimes also known as the magpie, is one of the newer varieties and gaining in popularity with goldfish keepers.*

Left: *From this viewing angle it is clear that the caudal fin of this young specimen is only 25% divided. Ideally, it should be fully divided, as in the more mature fish shown at far left.*

In Japan, the ranchu is possibly one of the most prized varieties of fancy goldfish and the Japanese standards for judging are very rigorous. The ranchu is very similar in appearance to the lionhead. However, the back is strongly arched, forming a sharp angle with the caudal fin and as a result, the caudal fin is orientated downwards. The absence of a dorsal fin, the shape of the other paired fins, and the wen (hood) are all similar to those of the lionhead.

Ranchus are metallic self-coloured orange, red-and-black or variegated, usually red-and-white (silver). Red-and-white nacreous varieties of ranchu – that is fish with a dull mother-of-pearl shine – are termed 'sakura nishiki', in Japan and calico nacreous are known as 'edo nishiki'.

An ideal 90° angle

Left: The most obvious feature of the profile of the ranchu is the absence of the dorsal fin. The back is steeply arched, while the tail fin faces almost downwards. There should be no evidence of a vestigial dorsal fin, such as a bump or depression where the fin should be. The angle between the caudal peduncle and the tail fin should be 90°.

This is a fine example of the breed.

Right: In this red-and-silver metallic ranchu, the red wen, or hood, can be seen covering the top of the head, spreading around the eyes and extending over the gill covers.

Right: This view shows that the tail fin is fully divided. Seen from the rear, the lobes of the tail should be held at 90° to each other.

Left: A side view of the ranchu pictured below it. Note the clean outline of the back, and the angle between the peduncle and the caudal. These are some of characteristics that judges will be looking for in a good fish.

Below: Numerous colour varieties of ranchu have been bred, including black. This is a particularly good specimen.

Below: A top view reveals a strong and chunky-bodied ranchu, with wen development in all three areas: the top of the head, around the eyes and over the gill covers.

Lionheads

Chinese lionhead were originally bred to look like the mythical lion dog. The body is round and very deep, the depth being at least half he body length in good-quality specimens. The back should curve gently and smoothly towards the tail. The pectoral, pelvic and anal fins are paired, as is the caudal fin, which should be clearly divided and forked. The tips of all the fins should be rounded. Lionheads have two notable characteristics. The first is the absence of the dorsal fin; there should be no spurs or any vestigial remnant of this fin. The second is the wen, or hood, which covers the top of the head and extends downwards and around the eyes and gill covers. The wen should not cover the eyes, but form a perfect hood around the head of the lionhead, giving it a very cute, chubby-cheeked appearance.

Lionheads are bred with calico or metallic self-coloured or variegated colours, which should extend into the fins. The pattern of the variegated lionheads should be balanced in an attractive pattern, which should be similar on each side of the body.

The pompon has a body shape and arrangement of fins similar to that described for the celestial and bubble-eye. Fish have two nostrils on either side of the head, interconnected by a U-shaped tube lined with special sensory cells that can detect very small amounts of any chemical in the water. In other words, their function is rather like that of the human nose, giving fish the ability to smell airborne chemicals or odours. A tiny flap of skin called the nasal septum, separates the two orifices that form the nostrils. In the pompon, the nasal septa have been developed into bunches of fleshy lobes, that resemble pompons. The pompons should be well developed but not sucked into the mouth as the fish breathes. They should be spherical in shape and rather solid in texture. Pompons are found both in metallic and calico colours.

Right: Chocolate pompons with dorsal fins. The fishes' nasal septa are in the form of fleshy lobes that look like raised pompons. In good-quality specimens, these should be equally developed.

Below: Good-quality calico pompons should have a blue background with patches of colour and be spotted with black. The dorsal fin is absent in true pompons.

The pearlscale is a very attractive and popular variety of goldfish. The body is almost spherical (like a golf ball). The head is quite pointed and small, with a petite mouth. The dorsal fin is single and all the other fins are paired and should be rounded at the tips. The caudal fin should be divided and the lobes forked (although nowhere near as much as in a fantail). The upper lobes should be held high and should not drop as the fish swims.

As the name suggests, the important feature of the pearlscale variety is its scales. These have a thickened area in the centre with a deposit of calcium carbonate that makes them dome-shaped and gives them the appearance of a pearl. There are metallic self-coloured and variegated or calico varieties of pearlscale, in which the colours should be very strong.

Although these hardy little fish can live outdoors in a garden pond, they are best kept in an aquarium, where they can be seen to best advantage.

Right: A calico variety of the pearlscale goldfish. This fine fish has a good colour and is a clear example of how the domed scales should look.

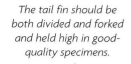
The tail fin should be both divided and forked and held high in good-quality specimens.

Left: *The pearlscale should have domed scales over the whole body surface, and the colours should extend from the body into the fins.*

Below: *A young red-and-white (silver) pearlscale, showing the calcium deposits beneath the scales that give this variety its distinctive appearance. In the best ones, the body is as wide as it is deep.*

Hama nishiki is a cross between the pearlscale and the oranda, although when judged in any shows, it is usually included in the category of 'any other varieties' (AOV). The body shape and scales of the hama nishiki are essentially like those of the pearlscale. The dorsal fin is single and all the others are paired, but slightly longer on the hama nishiki than the pearlscale. The main characteristic that distinguishes the hama nishiki from a pearlscale is the presence of a wen (hood) covering the top of the head. Overall, the hama nishiki is slightly larger than the pearlscale, growing to about 20cm (8in) long.

Left: The dome-shaped scales of this hama nishiki are clearly visible, as is the wen on top of the head. The wen development could be greater, but will probably increase as the fish matures.

The tail fin is divided and forked.

The body is deep and broad.

Left: In this example, the fins of the hama nishiki are longer than those of the pearlscale, but this is not always the case.

Right: This fish has very good pearling and well-balanced finnage, plus the pointed head required of the breed. New varieties and colour patterns are constantly being developed in the hobby.

GOLDFISH VARIETIES – CELESTIAL

The celestial tends to be one of the smaller varieties of fancy goldfish. The dorsal fin is absent and the back is gently sloping towards the caudal fin, which should be clearly divided and forked. All the other fins are paired and should have rounded edges. The body is deep, ideally at least half the body length, but the notable feature concerns the eyes, which not only protrude but face upwards. These spherical protuberances should be well developed and in good specimens of celestial are the same size, shape and coloration. Celestials occur as metallic self-coloured and variegated, and calico.

Celestials should be kept in an aquarium without strong lighting or any furniture on which they might injure their delicate eye tissue. For this reason they are probably not suitable for the novice fishkeeper.

Right: The celestial has no dorsal fin, but should show a smoothly arched back, as here. The caudal fins should not be too big or the body too long and shallow.

Below: The eyes of the celestial not only protrude from the body but must look upwards. In good-quality fish, they are equal in size.

GOLDFISH VARIETIES – BUBBLE-EYE

The bubble-eye's body shape and arrangement of fins are similar to that described for the celestial, but its distinguishing feature, as the name suggests, is the extreme development of fluid-filled pouches of skin under and around the eyes. Viewed from the side, the bubble-eye looks rather as if it is peeping over the top of the bubblelike pouch. As it swims, the pouches wobble in a characteristic fashion. In very good specimens of bubble-eye, the pouches are well developed and of a similar size and shape. Bubble-eyes may be calico or metallic self-coloured and variegated.

The skin surrounding the bubblelike pouch is easily damaged, particularly if internal filters are used in the aquarium. Keep the fish in a bare tank with no plants, gravel or ornaments on which it could injure itself. Not a fish for the novice fish keeper.

The tail should be divided and forked.

The 'bubble' is a fluid-filled pouch or sac that protrudes from beneath each eye.

Below: *The eyes do not protrude, but, like those of celestials, they look upwards and are situated above the fluid-filled pouches.*

Below: *Three self-coloured metallic bubble-eyes. The development of the bubble eyes is greatest in the middle specimen. The fish tend to be poor swimmers and are best kept in a separate aquarium from other fancy goldfish.*

Left: *In the bubble-eye, the dorsal fin is absent and the body should be smoothly contoured.*

INDEX

Page numbers in **bold** indicate major entries; *italics* refer to captions and annotations; plain type indicates other text entries.

CREDITS

The publishers would like to thank the following photographers for providing images, credited here by page number and position: B(Bottom), T(Top), C(Centre), BL(Bottom Left), etc.

Aqua Press: Title page, 6, 48; Dave Bevan: 27(BC, TR), 32(TR), 35(TR), 38(BL, T), 39, 42(C), 73(L); Dick Mills: 8(R); Aaron Norman: 68; Mike Pepper: 46; Photomax (Max Gibbs): 10(BL), 42(L), 52, 53(T), 54, 55, 58, 59, 64, 69, 70-71, 71(BR), 73(R), 75; Fred Rosenzweig: 71(BL); Neil Sutherland © Geoffrey Rogers Interpet Publishing: 27(BR), 28(BC).

All other photographs by Geoffrey Rogers © Interpet Publishing.

Illustrations by Stuart Watkinson © Interpet Publishing.

The publishers would like to thank Stephen J. Smith; Maureen McGurk at Koishii, Tewin, Welwyn, Herts; Dennis Roberts and Nick Fletcher.